Economic Effects of Exchange-Rate Changes

Economic Effects of Exchange-Rate Changes

Klaus-Walter Riechel

Lexington Books
D.C. Heath and Company
Lexington, Massachusetts
Toronto

Library of Congress Cataloging in Publication Data

Riechel, Klaus-Walter.
Economic effects of exchange-rate changes.

Bibliography: p.
Includes index.
1. Foreign exchange problem. 2. Balance of payments.
I. Title.
HG3826.R46 332.4′5 78–58926
ISBN 0–669–02376–0

Published simultaneously in Canada

Printed in the United States of America

International Standard Book Number: 0–669–02376–0

Library of Congress Catalog Card Number: 78–58926

Contents

List of Figures

Preface

On April 1, 1978, the Second Amendment to the International Monetary Fund's Articles of Agreement entered into force. The acceptance of the amendment by the required majority of the total voting power binds all 133 members of the Fund. The provisions with overriding importance in the Second Amendment pertain to the subject of exchange arrangements. Under the original Articles of Agreement, which were adopted in Bretton Woods in 1944, exchange-rate changes were permitted only in cases of "fundamental disequilibria"; under the new provisions member countries are free to apply the exchange arrangements of their choice. The adoption of the Second Amendment thereby legalizes the various forms of exchange regimes, other than the par system, that had become current practice since the collapse of the Bretton Woods system in 1971. Up to 1971 exchange-rate changes had, indeed, been a rather infrequent policy measure. After the 1971 devaluation of the dollar in terms of gold, exchange-rate changes in the form of either discrete steps or a continuous floating became a more frequent phenomenon. As a result, adjustments in exchange rates have gained considerable importance for both the design of domestic economic policies and the maintenance of international monetary stability.

The present study addresses itself chiefly to a comprehensive theoretical account of the effects of exchange-rate changes within a single economy. It adopts as a framework for analysis the "monetary approach to balance-of-payments adjustment" on the grounds that this approach (1) constitutes a general, rather than a partial, equilibrium approach, and that it (2) contains an automatic adjustment mechanism and, thereby, overcomes the implicit assumption of earlier approaches that—if not corrected by policy measures—a balance-of-payments disequilibrium can last forever. The analyses generally describe the effects of discrete changes in the exchange rate out of an equilibrium situation. This appears at first sight to severely limit the use of the results derived in this study. It has to be borne in mind, however, that a policy which fixes the exchange rate above its equilibrium value or one which through a "dirty float" keeps the exchange rate of the domestic currency undervalued will induce adjustment processes in the private sector very similar to those brought about by a devaluation. Therefore, if adopted correctly and interpreted carefully, the results of the analyses presented in this study will be relevant for a wide range of exchange arrangements and policies.

The present study constitutes a rather comprehensive account of a rigorous application of the fundamental assumptions and concepts of the monetary approach to the balance of payments to a disaggregated sectoral analysis of exchange-rate changes. Like many other comprehensive studies, it incorporates a good many ideas developed by others. Where appropriate this has been acknowledged in the text. In addition to inspirations from ideas that have been put down in writing, I have benefited a great deal from private correspondence and discussions with a large number of friends, colleagues, and teachers. My special appreciation and sincere thanks belong to Professors Manfred Willms and Jürgen Rohwedder, both of the Christian-Albrechts-Universität in Kiel, West Germany, whose invaluable comments and criticisms of an earlier version of this study helped to achieve greater consistency in the presentation and eliminated a number of mistakes.

The study was completed while I was affiliated with the Christian-Albrechts-Universität Kiel. The views and opinions expressed are mine and in no way reflect those of the International Monetary Fund or any of its officials.

Economic Effects of Exchange-Rate Changes

1 Exchange-Rate Changes as a Policy Instrument

It is common wisdom that the exchange rate is a price. It is not, however, just one price among others such as the price of needles or apples; it is a very different price. The importance of the exchange rate as a price derives from two special features. The first feature concerns the range of influence of a change in this price. A change in the price of apples exerts an influence almost solely on the market for apples and possibly on the markets for close substitutes such as pears and peaches; all other markets remain essentially unaffected. Furthermore, since apples are just one item in the basket of goods consumed by the community and, therefore, the share of expenditures on apples in total expenditure is relatively small, real income and wealth will remain essentially unchanged by a rise in the price of apples. On the other hand, a variation in the exchange rate changes the price of a national money in terms of foreign monies. It thereby produces instantaneous disequilibria in all markets for exportable and importable commodities and services, as well as in the markets for internationally tradable assets. A wide range of prices will respond to these disequilibria, and this will usually not remain without consequences for the general national price level. Variations in the general price level, in turn, affect real incomes and real wealth of the community as a whole. The exchange rate is, consequently, a price of overriding importance for any economy. Changes in this price can be expected to produce adjustment processes of quite a different nature and quality than variations in the price of any single commodity.

It is therefore not surprising that the exchange rate has gained a strategic position in economic policy and that policymakers are quite reluctant to leave the determination of this price entirely to market forces. This fact constitutes the second special feature of the exchange rate as a price: it is a price which has almost always been subject to varying degrees of manipulation by economic policymakers. Periods during which the determination of the exchange rate has been left entirely to market forces are rare and usually of short duration.

During the period of the gold standard, policymakers decided to artificially fix the price of their currencies in terms of gold. Since gold was the numeraire for all currencies, this policy simultaneously determined all exchange rates between national monies and rendered them invariably fixed. By so doing, countries chose to ignore the fact that different economic developments among countries would lead to different developments in the purchasing power of national monies and would, thereby, normally require an adjustment in the relative price of national monies, i.e., a change in the exchange rate. By fixing exchange rates, the adjustment toward equilibrium was forced to take the form of variations in national price levels.[1]

The classical approach to balance-of-payments analysis, generally referred to as the Humean "price-specie-flow mechanism," describes the way in which the required adjustment is brought about. Neglecting capital movements, flows of goods and services are expected to respond to differences in prices among economies. Changes in relative price levels affect the direction and volume of goods flows and thereby create differences in foreign receipts and payments which are offset by gold flows. These gold flows enlarge the volume of assets backing the money stock in one country and deplete it in another country. Aggregate money supply is correspondingly changed in both countries; given the level of output, this produces an adjustment in the respective national price levels in an opposite direction. The corresponding change in relative prices, in turn, affects the demand for imports and exports such that the balance-of-payments adjustment clearly involves an automaticity in the adjustment to an imbalance.

A fundamental prerequisite for the automaticity of adjustment is the flexibility of prices. The degree of flexibility of prices, in turn, is a close function of the flexibility of the costs of production, notably of labor costs. The flexibility of nominal wages had been rather high until about the middle of the nineteenth century. The balance-of-payments adjustment process was, therefore, indeed automatic and occurred without major frictions. Various political and economic developments, in particular the emergence of trade unions, led, however, to a rather substantial decline in the downward flexibility of the wage component in total costs of production. This development produced a shift in the burden of adjustment due to imbalances in the foreign accounts from price adjustments to quantity adjustments. A reduction in the domestic money supply, as a result of a balance-of-payments deficit, for example, tended to produce unemployment and a corresponding decline in output rather than an immediate adjustment in prices and wages. The amount and duration of unemployment increased with a decline in the flexibility of wages and prices. Output of countries was, as of then, seriously affected by imbalances in the foreign accounts. This was particularly true for deficit countries. The gold standard, therefore, possessed a deflationary bias.

The experience with the gold standard under a relative rigidity of wages in the downward direction made countries more and more aware of the apparent conflict between national policy goals and the requirements for external balance. Countries became increasingly unwilling to subordinate their national policy goals to the requirements of balance-of-payments equilibrium. The mass unemployment experienced by all industrialized countries in the late 1920s and early 1930s produced a dramatic shift in opinion as to the practicability and appropriateness of the regulations under which the gold standard operated.

In order to cope with their unemployment and balance-of-payments problems, several countries suspended their currencies from the gold standard and turned to exchange-rate depreciations in the hope of improving their international competitive position and thereby stimulate international demand for domestic products. Some of the effective depreciations, such as the devaluation of the pound sterling in 1931/32, proved to be quite successful in improving the trade balance and in alleviating the problem of unemployment. The positive effects of a devaluation on the devaluating countries and the negative effects on their trading partners (beggar-my-neighbor policy) produced, however, a series of competitive devaluations which tended to cancel each other. In spite of this development, the exchange rate became an economic policy variable of central importance.

The breakdown of the gold standard and the series of exchange-rate changes in the 1930s produced a strand of literature on the international adjustment process under the new system. Central to the theoretical investigations was the case of a change in the exchange rate. The result of these investigations was not comforting. A devaluation, rather than improving the trade balance, could easily lead to its deterioration. Only if demand and supply elasticities took certain minimum values would a devaluation lead to an improvement in the trade balance.[2] The first empirical tests on the respective elasticities proved to be disquieting in that they suggested that a devaluation would more likely than not result in a deterioration of the trade balance. An elasticity pessimism arose. Countries by and large abstained from exchange-rate depreciations.

The elasticity approach was soon criticized by a number of economists as being partial equilibrium in nature. The approach examines variations in trade flows in response to price changes as the only determinants of these flows; all other variables are assumed to be constant. In addition, the approach neglects capital flows. Given the importance of the exchange rate as a price, this treatment is clearly unsatisfactory and yields misleading results.

Several attempts were made to overcome the partial equilibrium nature of the elasticity approach by adding to the equation system central economic variables other than prices as determinants of demand for and supply of imports and exports. Apart from becoming overly complex and complicated, these approaches still neglected a central explanatory variable for the exchange rate—money. This criticism also applies largely to the Keynesian-type "international trade multiplier theory."

While the debate among economists about the values of elasticities and analytical ways of improving on the elasticity approach continued, the international community had installed a new international monetary system. The planners of the so-called Bretton Woods system were clearly impressed by the experience with the international monetary system in the interwar period. A return to the gold standard was considered inappropriate since it would again subjugate domestic economic policy objectives to balance-of-payments considerations. On the other hand, a system of freely fluctuating exchange rates was believed to be inherently unstable and therefore detrimental to the expansion of international trade, the international division of labor, and the optimal allocation of resources.

For these reasons, the planners of the Bretton Woods system sought to compromise on the two polar systems: they aimed at preserving a great amount of stability of the exchange rate, while at the same time allowing for infrequent and discrete changes in the exchange rate.

This arrangement indicates that the exchange rate was given a dominant role in the new system: domestic policy measures which aimed at income adjustments were largely rejected as a vehicle for international adjustment. Therefore, variations in the exchange rate were the central device for bringing a country back to a stable development once its balance of payments was in a "fundamental disequilibrium." Contrary to theorists who adhered to the fraternity of "elasticity pessimists," the planners of the Bretton Woods system obviously believed in the efficacy of exchange-rate changes as a device for correcting disequilibria in the external balances.

The regulations on exchange-rate changes in the Bretton Woods agreements were, however, rather rigid, on the one hand, and flimsy, on the other. In order to avoid a series of competitive exchange-rate changes like the ones in the 1930s, changes in the exchange rate were permitted only if they were to correct a "fundamental disequilibrium." Though it was believed that in practice a situation which constituted a fundamental disequilibrium could be recognized, the meaning of the term was never clearly defined. As a result, countries which found themselves in a situation of balance-of-payments disequilibrium had no means to decide whether a change in the exchange rate was required or not. At the same time, the International Monetary Fund, which was to oversee the international monetary system, had no unambiguous measure by which it could recommend or press for an adjustment in the exchange rate of individual member countries. In practice, therefore, countries decided on the grounds of national priorities whether to change the exchange rate. Little notice was generally taken of the requirements for a smooth working of the international monetary system as a whole and its stability. This type of behavior by certain countries was facilitated—in particular for deficit countries—by the arrangements of the Bretton Woods system itself. The regulations of the Bretton Woods system envisaged that short- and medium-term disequilibria be handled by transfers in international reserves. For this purpose a comprehensive system of international credit and standby arrangements was gradually installed and expanded. The regulations were such that deficit countries had almost automatic access to credit. Contrary to the intentions of the founders of the Bretton Woods system, these arrangements in practice often meant that countries obtained massive credits for extended periods of time, much longer than envisaged for the financing of a temporary disequilibrium.

Deficit countries were, consequently, hardly forced to take steps to correct the imbalance in their external accounts by either restrictive domestic policy measures or exchange-rate changes. Surplus countries, on the other hand, mostly abstained from appreciation of their currencies in order not to endanger the competitive edge of their export industries and in fear of ensuing unemployment. This behavior on the part of deficit and surplus countries attributed an inflationary bias to the system which became visible and felt, however, only as output of the industrialized world approached its full-employment level.

More serious than the inflationary bias in the system was, however, that it failed to provide for an operative "automatic" adjustment mechanism: there were no clear-cut rules for more or less automatic adjustments in exchange rates and no inescapable mechanism or need for corrective domestic policy measures. Given the behavior of central banks and fiscal authorities, the system was bound to fail sooner or later.

In the theoretical debate on the mechanism of international adjustment, economic science took a big step forward at a time when the discussion about the values of elasticities and the extension of the elasticity approach had reached a stalemate. In 1952, Sidney S. Alexander introduced a new approach to devaluation analysis.[3] Rather than confining itself to a country's quantitative economic relations with other economies, this approach draws attention to the importance of its aggregate income and expenditure. The balance of payments is seen to be the difference between the flow of income of an economy and its expenditure.[4] Alexander states that a devaluation, if it is to succeed, requires an adjustment in either or both of these two variables: a rise in income (output) and a decline in expenditure. The so-called absorption approach proved to be pathbreaking for and an integral part of modern approaches to balance-of-payments adjustment. The absorption approach does not yet contain an automaticity in the adjustment to a disturbance of the economic system. Rather, domestic policy measures will generally be required to go along with a change in the exchange rate in order to bring about the desired changes in the balance of payments.

It is the merit of the monetary approach to the balance of payments[5] to have developed an intellectually appealing theoretical framework which points to those elements inherent in the economic system which ensure an automatic adjustment in response to external shocks such as changes in the exchange rate. Like many other models of a different provenance, the models of the proponents of the monetary approach to balance-of-payments analysis generally contain a limited set of well-specified behavioral equations and identities to describe the complex interdependencies in an economy. It is a special feature of the monetary approach, however, that it concentrates on the long run and that it assumes passivity of action on the part of the monetary authorities in the interrun.

The focus of attention of this study will be somewhat different. It will concern itself primarily with describing the short- and medium-run disequilibria that arise in various markets after a change in the exchange rate. It will then concentrate on a few central variables which are affected by exchange-rate changes, examine the direction in which they must be expected to move and to what extent, and finally will analyze the consequences of adjustments which the public and the authorities can be expected to make in response to variations in these variables. Particular interest will be devoted to the behavior of the authorities. It is asserted that, though not entirely unconcerned with the long-run development of their economies, the authorities tend to focus their attention on the short- and medium-run perspectives and "requirements" of economic policy. Short- and medium-run disequilibria in important markets are then likely to induce adjustments in economic policy measures. If this behavioral pattern exists, it is necessary to spell out the kind and importance of short- and medium-run disequilibria which arise as a result of exchange-rate changes. From the type and importance of these disequilibria it should be possible to find out which policy measures are most likely to be implemented in response to these disequilibria. Finally, it should be possible to judge the implications of these measures for the success of exchange-rate changes.

A detailed study of short- and medium-run phenomena related to exchange-rate changes should also help to answer questions such as why the devaluation of the pound sterling in 1931/32 was quite successful in improving the trade balance, while the British devaluations in the late 1960s and early 1970s did not show any significant success.

The study is organized along the following lines: In Chapter 2, the study will begin with a brief review of the essential features of the monetary approach to balance-of-payments analysis. It will then lay the foundations for the application of the Archibald-Lipsey model[6] to an economy as a whole and demonstrate the adjustment process after a devaluation. The analysis will proceed with an enlargement of the wealth concept by first introducing nontradable bonds. This adjustment will allow for an analysis of interest effects on the utility-maximizing choices open to the public and on the path of adjustment of the economy. The next section will introduce tradable bonds and thereby abandon the restriction of the international adjustment process to adjustments in the trade balance. In addition to movements in the trade balance, both adjustments in the capital and service accounts will be demonstrated.

Chapter 3 concentrates on portfolio adjustments in a three-asset model in response to variations in the exchange rate. Particular emphasis will be given to the interaction between interest rates, spending behavior, financing requirements, and portfolio adjustment.

Chapter 4 turns to the adjustment process in the commodity markets. Various assumptions about price and wage behavior as well as about alternative reactions of the authorities will be considered.

Chapter 5 and 6 will direct attention to the not unrelated problems of money illusion and price expectations. The implications of either the absence or presence of money illusion and of various assumptions about price expectations will be investigated and their effects described.

Chapter 7 will summarize the results and discuss the policy implications yielded by the present study.

The analysis of the economic effects of exchange-rate changes will generally start from a situation of overall equilibrium. This is, of course, a situation in which it is unlikely that the authorities will decide to change the exchange rate.[7] The above approach has, however, the advantage of a much greater degree of clarity than an approach which starts from the more realistic assumption of an initial disequilibrium. The direction and relative size of the impact of a change in the exchange rate as well as of the subsequent adjustment process remain unaffected by this simplification.

2 Devaluation, Wealth, and Spending

The Basic Monetary Approach to Balance-of-Payments Adjustment

The monetary approach to the balance of payments emphasizes three fundamental principles.[1] The first of these principles is that the balance of payments is essentially a monetary phenomenon. The second states the importance of both a stable money-supply process and a stable money-demand function. Finally the monetary approach concentrates on "the longer-run consequences of policy and parametric changes for the behavior of the balance of payments."[2] These rather general principles require more specific explanations in order to set the stage for a detailed analysis of the effects of exchange-rate changes as a monetary phenomenon.

A problem related to the proposition that the balance of payments is an essentially monetary phenomenon is to determine the appropriate concept of the balance of payments. The monetary approach asserts that the various definitions of the balance of payments which focus on subbalances or groupings of subbalances are inappropriate for the analysis of the balance of payments in a general equilibrium context. These definitions, in order to be operative, require the formulation of behavioral relationships which are generally unable to encompass all variables relevant to the adjustment process. As such they are bound to lead to approaches to balance-of-payments adjustment which are partial equilibrium in nature. However, as stated in chapter 1, it has been the partial equilibrium nature of early approaches, such as the elasticity approach, which has led to the search for ways to avoid this shortcoming. As a result the monetary approach relies on the balance of payments in its most comprehensive definition, namely, as the sum of the items "below the line," i.e., the "balance of official settlements."[3] Since any imbalance in this account (B) is identical to a change in the country's international reserves (R),

$$B = \frac{dR}{dt} \tag{2.1}$$

it is not difficult to see in which sense the balance of payments is an essentially monetary phenomenon.

International reserves form one part of the monetary base (MB) backing the domestic money supply, the other part being net domestic assets of the central bank (D). Therefore,

$$MB = D + R \tag{2.2}$$

Abstracting from sterilization operations of the central bank, a change in the volume of international reserves will, in a system of fixed exchange rates, uno actu vary the potential for monetary expansion in the country concerned.

This leads to the first part of the second essential feature of the monetary approach: the assumption of a stable money-supply process. If it were conceivable that a change in the monetary base would over a longer period of time in no way affect the money supply, then a given change in international reserves would not initiate any adjustment in the behavior of the public since the balance between money demand and money supply would remain undisturbed. On the other hand, a stable multiplicative relationship between the monetary base and the money supply guarantees that a given change in the monetary base is always translated into a multiple change in the money supply and, hence, leads to a disequilibrium in the money market.

Assume that the money multiplier (φ) is constant in the long run. The money supply is then determined by[4]

$$M = \varphi\, MB = \varphi\,(D + R) \tag{2.3}$$

and the change in the money supply by

$$\frac{dM}{dt} = \varphi \frac{dMB}{dt} = \varphi \left(\frac{dD}{dt} + \frac{dR}{dt} \right) \tag{2.4}$$

In the absence of active, offsetting domestic monetary policy, dD/dt is equal to zero and equation (2.4) is transformed into the relation between the change in international reserves and the money supply.

$$\frac{dM}{dt} = \varphi \frac{dR}{dt} \tag{2.5}$$

The other source of an imbalance in the money market is a variation in the demand for money. The monetary approach postulates that the public's demand for money is a stable function of a limited number of variables such as income, interest rates, and the price level.

$$L = L\,(Y,i,P, \ldots) \qquad (2.6)$$

In the stationary state these variables do not change and, consequently, neither does money demand. In a growing economy, money demand develops in a fixed proportion to the equilibrium growth of income, prices, etc.

The importance of a stable money-demand function is easily demonstrated by the following example: assume an autonomous increase in domestic credit via a minimum-reserves policy of the central bank. Given a stable money multiplier the domestic money supply will increase by a multiple of this increase in the monetary base. In the absence of a stable money-demand function, this increase will not lead to an equiproportionate excess supply of money. In the extreme case the entire amount of the additional money supply will be willingly absorbed by the public and no further change in economic variables will result from this behavior.[5] While admitting fluctuations in money demand in the short run, the monetary approach denies the possibility of such a behavior in the long run. An increasing number of empirical investigations have indeed shown that the demand for money is highly stable in the long run, "more stable than functions such as the consumption function that are offered as alternative key relations."[6]

Empirical investigations also show that the supply of money has in the longer run followed changes in the monetary base in a rather close and predictable fashion, thereby proving the existence of a stable money multiplier, and thus of a stable money-supply process.[7]

The analysis of short-run data, on the other hand, generally provides evidence that both money demand and money supply follow an often erratic and rather unpredictable pattern. This explains the emphasis of the monetary approach on long-run analysis.

Two basic questions have been left open in reviewing the fundamental features of the monetary approach. The first is the question, What determines the net position of all the items "above the line"? In other words, what determines the magnitude of the balance of payments defined as the change of international reserves? The second is the way in which an imbalance in the money market translates itself into "real behavior" of the public. As will be shown below the two questions are related.

The first question is partly answered by reference to the key relationship (or identity) of the absorption approach, according to which a balance-of-payments surplus requires an excess of domestic income over domestic absorption (expenditure).[8] Concentrating at first on the balance of trade (as does the absorption approach) this relation can be expressed by

$$\frac{B}{P} \equiv \frac{dR}{Pdt} = y - a, \qquad (2.7)$$

where P is the price level and hence B/P is the real balance-of-payments surplus; y is real income and a is real absorption (expenditure on goods). The question of what determines the balance of payments can then be rephrased as the question of what determines real income and real absorption.

It is commonly assumed in monetary models that both flexibility in prices and wages and factor mobility exists in the long run. This ensures that the economy will always be producing at its full-employment level. Full-employment income is then given by the level of existing resources and technology in a stationary economy, and by the equilibrium growth of these variables in a growing economy.

Given real income, the balance of payments is consequently determined by variations in real domestic absorption. Thus, the analysis of balance-of-payments adjustment requires as another key element a theory about absorption behavior. A number of different absorption functions have recently been proposed;[9] all of them stress, however, the importance of monetary factors in determining real behavior.

The simplest version of an absorption function, and one which closes directly the circle of the highly aggregated model of balance-of-payments adjustment espoused by the monetary approach, relates absorption to the difference between actual real cash balances and desired real balances. In this version real absorption is equal to real income plus a part of any discrepancy between actual and desired real cash balances.

$$a = y + \lambda\left(\frac{M}{P} - \frac{L}{P}\right) \tag{2.8}$$

λ is an adjustment coefficient which has a "per-unit-of-time" dimension. Given real income, absorption in any period will depend on the magnitude of the real excess demand for money and the velocity with which the economy decides to close the gap between desired and actual real balances. λ will therefore be called "absorption velocity."[10] If λ equals unity, adjustment to an imbalance in the money market will be instantaneous. In the case of $0 < \lambda < 1$, adjustment will be spread over more than one period.

Since both real money demand and real money supply relate to a stock magnitude, equation (2.8) may be viewed as a functional relationship describing a stock-adjustment process. On the other hand, equality of real money balances demanded and supplied at any point in time defines flow equilibrium in the goods markets.

It should be noticed that equation (2.8) contains an implicit saving function of the type suggested by Metzler in his celebrated article, "Wealth, Saving, and the Rate of Interest."[11] The value of real saving of the economy as a whole is given by[12]

$$s = y - a = -\lambda\left(\frac{M}{P} - \frac{L}{P}\right) \tag{2.9}$$

Saving can thus be viewed as a process of wealth accumulation aimed at the maximization of some intertemporal utility function which contains both a flow argument, i.e., consumption, and a stock argument, i.e., real money balances or, more generally, real wealth.[13] With the addition of equation (2.8) to the set of equations advanced before, the simplest of all monetary models of balance-of-payments adjustment is complete. It is easily demonstrated that the model is closed in the sense that it generates an automatic adjustment process.[14] Initial equilibrium is given by the equality of actual real-cash balances and their desired quantity. Accordingly, as is witnessed by equation (2.8) real absorption will be exactly equal to real income, net real saving will be equal to zero. As a result the balance of payments will also be zero [compare equation (2.7)].

Assume now a disturbance in the balance between real-money demand and supply causing an excess demand for money. By equation (2.8) absorption will decline below real income. The resulting excess supply of domestically produced goods is absorbed by demand from the rest of the world, which, by virtue of the small-country assumption, is infinitely elastic. As a result, the home country will experience a surplus in the balance of payments [compare equation (2.7)]. The corresponding flow supply of reserves, equation (2.1), leads to an expansion in the monetary base, equation (2.2), which is translated via a multiplicative process, equations (2.3), (2.4), or (2.5) into a multiple increase in the money supply. This increase serves to reduce the initial excess demand for money. The process will continue until actual real balances are again built up to their desired level.

This description of the adjustment mechanism demonstrates once again the importance of the basic features of the monetary approach. Without the focus on the long run, there would be no empirically backed reason to assume a stable money-demand function and money-supply process. As a result, a disturbance in the system need not affect an imbalance between actual and desired real-cash balances. Consequently, the disturbance would not a priori generate a change in spending behavior and thus in the balance between real income and absorption. Hence, the balance of payments could conceivably remain unaffected. Without viewing the balance of payments as an essentially monetary phenomenon and defining it as the change in international reserves, the direct or feedback effect of the balance of payments on monetary equilibrium would be obscured and, hence, the automaticity of the adjustment process would be broken. It is crucial to understanding the monetary approach that the economy cannot be in full stock-and-flow equilibrium unless the balance of payments is in equilibrium, i.e., unless $dR/dt = 0$. Any balance-of-payments surplus or deficit will affect the domestic money supply and will thus lead to an adjustment in spending decisions which, in turn, will create flow disequilibria.

After having described the monetary approach of balance-of-payments analysis in its most general form, it is now possible to dwell upon some of the more important details of the basic equation system.

The Archibald-Lipsey Framework and Devaluation Analysis

The presentation of the simple monetary model of balance-of-payments analysis revealed that the achievement of full stock-and-flow equilibrium in an economy involves interdependent adjustments in stocks and flows. It is obvious that the observed changes in the variables which adjust to disturbances, as well as the magnitudes of the stock and flow variables which obtain in full equilibrium, will not be of an arbitrary size. Rather, they are expected to be determined by utility-maximization considerations of economic agents. It is this fundamental concept which will be applied to the derivation of an algebraic and graphic framework for the analysis of exchange-rate changes in this section.

Society may be assumed to derive direct and indirect utility from both real income/absorption and real balances. A thorough analysis of the factors underlying and influencing the decision-making processes involved in the quest for utility maximization is paramount for answering a series of questions in connection with the monetary approach to balance-of-payments analysis presented above. These questions are:

1. Which fundamental forces determine the desired level of real balances of an economy? Furthermore, can this level be expected to be constant in the long run in the case of a stationary economy, and to grow at a given rate in a growing economy?
2. If it can be assumed that a well-defined desired level of real balances exists, which forces determine the path and speed of adjustment after a disturbance?
3. Under which conditions will an automatic adjustment process get underway? Will it follow a stable path and lead to a stable equilibrium?

In this section the investigation of the above questions in general and their importance for an analysis of exchange-rate changes in particular will be cast in a framework which incorporates all essential elements of the monetary approach to balance-of-payments analysis. The analysis will initially focus on an economy in which money is the only financial asset and in which economic relations with the rest of the world are restricted to the exchange of goods and money. In the next section nontraded bonds will be introduced as a second financial asset and the importance of this assumption for the path and speed of adjustment will be analyzed. In the last section it will be assumed that domestic bonds become internationally tradable. The repercussions of this assumption for the adjustment process will be spelled out in some detail.

The approach presented below will put special emphasis on the clarification of interdependencies between stock-and-flow adjustments. The main tool of this framework is a diagram developed by G.C. Archibald and R.G. Lipsey for their analysis of an individual's behavior in response to variations in either his actual or desired real balances.[15]

The analysis will first state the assumptions and make the adjustments required for an application of the Archibald-Lipsey diagram to an economy as a whole rather than to an individual.[16] It will then investigate the adjustment process after a devaluation and analyze the dynamic properties of the adjustment.

A General Determination of Desired Real Balances

One of the centerpieces of the Archibald-Lipsey analysis is the assumption of an indifference system which determines for each level of total resources, i.e., real income plus real balances, the utility-maximizing allocation of an individual's resources between consuming goods and holding real balances. The analysis implies that for any given level of real income there exists a unique level of real balances desired by economic agents.

It has been demonstrated in an abundance of articles that it is generally not possible to derive behavioral properties for an economy as a whole by aggregating over the total population information obtained from individuals' behavior. The application of the Archibald-Lipsey framework to the analysis of behavioral patterns of an economy as a whole therefore requires an investigation into the relation between an economy's income and absorption, on the one hand, and its desired level of real balances, on the other. This analysis will, at the same time, shed some light on one of the basic assumptions of the monetary approach of balance-of-payments analysis, namely, the assumption of an aggregate money-demand function which is stable in a limited number of variables[17] of which real income is the most prominent. It is of particular importance for the analysis of the effects of exchange-rate changes to investigate whether the exchange rate is one of the variables which influences desired real balances. Both the adjustment process and the final stock-flow equilibrium will crucially depend upon the answer to this question. For short-term policy purposes it is important to know whether a change in the exchange rate will involve a smooth or an erratic adjustment process, a stable or an unstable equilibrium.

The determination of the desired level of real balances is necessarily related to the fulfillment of some maximum criteria associated with the existence of money in an economy. The two general concepts which have been employed in order to investigate the role of money in an economy are the treatment of money as a producer's good and as a consumer's good.[18] In the first case, real money balances enter the production function. The maximum condition to be fulfilled therefore concerns the level of output of an economy. In the latter case, money balances appear as an argument in the aggregate utility function of consumers. Hence, it is utility derived from holding money balances which is to be maximized.

Consider first the role of money as a producer's good. For the sake of simplicity of presentation, and without loss of generality, assume in this section a closed economy. In order to clarify the influence of money on the economy and, in particular, its relation to other factors of production and output, the economy is assumed initially to be in the state of barter. Output is produced with two factors of production, labor, L, and capital, K, by way of a linear homogeneous production function.

$$y = f(L,K) \tag{2.10}$$

Given the supply of factors of production and technology, the economy will produce a certain given level of output.

Assume now that money is introduced into the economy and enters the production function, so that

$$y = g(L,K,M/P) \tag{2.11}$$

Output is again assumed to be linearly homogeneous in all variables.

The introduction of real balances into the production function may be seen to increase output of commodities in either of two ways. On the one hand, it may free either or both labor and capital for the production of commodities. Thus, resources which have formerly been devoted to achieving "the multitude of 'double coincidences'—of buyers who want exactly what the seller has to offer"[19] can now be employed in production proper. Alternatively, real-money balances may be seen to enter the production function in the form of disembodied technical progress of the Hicksian neutral variety, thus raising the productivity of both labor and capital by an equal but decreasing amount as money balances are increased. The latter approach can be analyzed in the following way:

Divide equation (2.11) by K to yield

$$\bar{y} \equiv \frac{y}{K} = h\left(\frac{L}{K}, 1, \frac{M}{PK}\right) \tag{2.12}$$

In a stationary economy the capital-labor ratio is a constant; thus, equation (2.12) may be rewritten in the following way:

$$\bar{y} \equiv \frac{y}{K} = k\left(\frac{M}{PK}\right) \equiv k(\bar{m}) \tag{2.13}$$

The capital-output ratio is, hence, exclusively a function of the real-balance-per-unit-of-capital ratio. Linear homogeneity implies that

$$\frac{\delta y}{\delta M/P} = \frac{\delta \bar{y}}{\delta \bar{m}} \equiv k'(\bar{m}) \tag{2.14}$$

and equally that

$$k'(\bar{m}) > 0 \text{ and } k''(\bar{m}) < 0 \tag{2.15}$$

Figure 2-1 depicts equation (2.13) under the assumption that equations (2.14) and (2.15) hold and that the premoney barter economy had extended its capital stock—given the labor force—until the marginal productivity of capital was equal to the marginal rate of time preference.[20] Given the initial capital stock K_0, the capital-output ratio of the barter economy is indicated by the level $\bar{y}_0$ on the ordinate of figure 2-1; the corresponding marginal productivity of capital is given by MPK_0

Assume now that money is introduced in the economy. For simplicity assume, furthermore, that during the entire process of monetization of the economy the marginal cost of producing money is equal to zero and that the monetary authorities allocate money to residents of the economy at no cost. This assumption avoids the complications of the difference between social and private costs of obtaining and holding money balances. At the same time there exists for the public neither a need to forego present consumption nor a need to substitute the capital stock in order to obtain additional real balances. The introduction of money raises the marginal product of the given stock of capital at a declining rate as depicted by the *MPK*-line starting at MPK_0; output per unit of capital increases as indicated by the $\bar{y}$-line starting at $\bar{y}_0$. As the money supply approaches the level M_1 at which the real-balance-to-capital ratio is $\bar{m}_1$, the marginal productivities of real balances, *MPM,* and of capital, *MPK,* converge and are ultimately equalized at point Q in figure 2-1.

Let the monetary authorities now increase the supply of money further so that the real-balance-to-capital ratio is given by $\bar{m}_2$. As the money stock increases to the level implied by $\bar{m}_2$, the marginal product of real balances declines to a level indicated by T, and the marginal product of capital increases to a level expressed by point S. Since the marginal product of capital now exceeds that of real balances, an incentive exists to substitute the former for the latter. By the assumption of a stationary economy, the capital stock is fixed. The aggregate attempt to purchase capital will therefore result in an increase in its price, P_k, and thereby raise the relative price of capital in terms of consumption goods, $d = P_k/P$, and lower its inverse, the yield on real capital, $r = P/P_k$. Given the marginal rate of time preference of the community, this rise in the relative price of future over present consumption will result in an increase in expenditure on

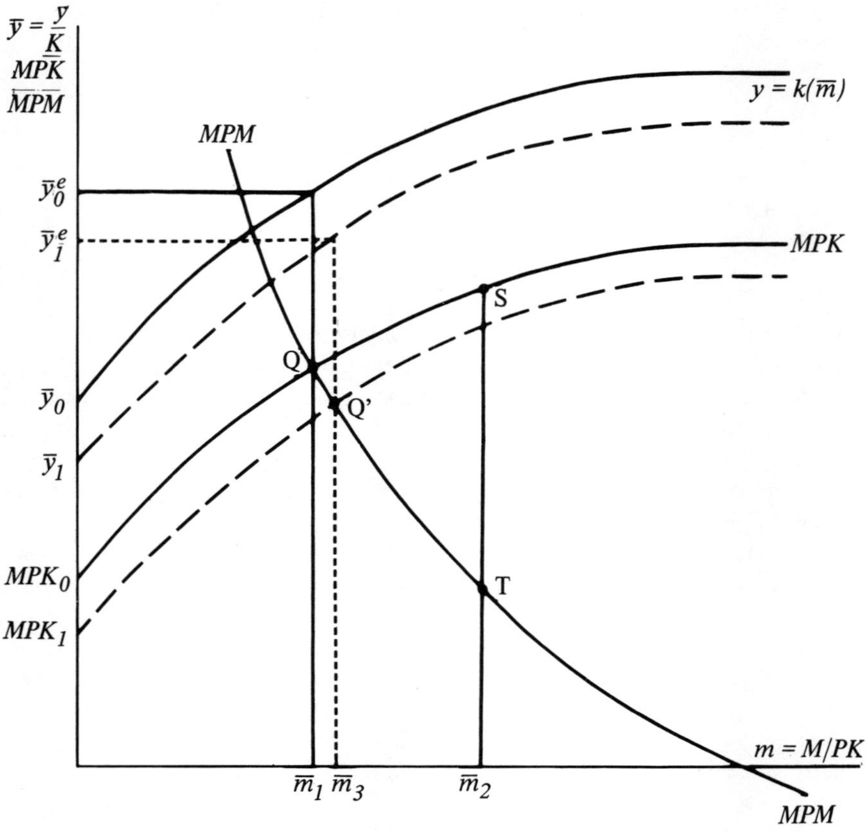

Figure 2–1. Optimality with Money as a Producer's Good.

present consumption which, in turn, will lead to an increase in the general price level. As P rises, real balances decline so that the real-balance-to-capital ratio approaches its former level $\bar{m}_1$. As long as the marginal productivity of capital exceeds the marginal productivity of real balances the yield on real capital will fall short of the marginal rate of time preference and, hence, favor present over future consumption: the price level will continue to rise. Equilibrium is restored at Q where the two marginal productivities are equal again and the general price level has risen by the percentage increase in the money supply, thus restoring the old real-balance-to-capital ratio $\bar{m}_1$.[21]

The above analysis demonstrates that if money is treated as a factor of production its desired level is determined by the equality of its own marginal product and that of capital. This finding is in no way different from the theorems suggested by general production theory. Given at any point in time the capital stock, the size of the labor force, technology and productivity of labor, given also the time preference of the community, there exists a unique level of real balances which maximizes utility over time via its influence on present and future output and, thus, consumption. In a stationary economy all of the above data are given and invariably fixed. The desired level of real balances is, in that case, seen to be a given and stable fraction of real income

$$l = ky \tag{2.16}$$

Consider now the role of money as a consumer's good. Real money balances enter the utility function because they are supposed to yield a flow of services to the individual holder and thus add to utility over and above the utility derived from the flow of consumption goods (a = absorption); hence, the utility function is denoted by[22]

$$U = U(a,z), \tag{2.17}$$

where z equals the flow of services derived from holdings of real money balances. Equation (2.17) indicates that money is not attributed a direct utility but only an indirect or derived utility. This utility may stem from a number of services provided by real balances. In a more recent approach, money is supposed to yield services via a reduction of transactors' costs of acquiring reliable information and also via a reduction of the variance of exchange ratios and thus a reduction of uncertainty about bundles of goods obtained in market exchange.[23] In the absence of money the individual would have to devote resources in the form of physical goods and labor to searching activities in order to reach the same level of information he or she has in a monetary economy. Thus, in a world of uncertainty the introduction of money increases welfare since it increases expected wealth and leisure time.[24]

For an economy as a whole the introduction of a standardized asset such as money also allows for a better allocation of resources between prospective savers and investors.[25] In the presence of money, specialized financial intermediaries can exploit economies of scale in lending and borrowing operations. At the same time, specialized traders can exploit economies of scale by acquiring knowledge about kind, quality, and prices of commodities in circulation.[26] The above reasoning suggests that, given the quantity of commodities, the additional services yielded by real balances decline as real balances increase so that

$$z = z(m) \text{ with } z'(m) > 0 \text{ and } z''(m) < 0, \tag{2.18}$$

where $m = M/P$.

By an appropriate choice of units, real balances can appear directly as an argument of the utility function so that

$$U = U(a,m) \text{ with } U'_a, U'_m > 0 \text{ and } U''_a, U''_m < 0 \qquad (2.19)$$

where U'_i and U''_i are the first and second derivatives respectively of the arguments in the utility function, indicating diminishing marginal utility from both absorpotion and real balances.

Equation (2.19) is represented in figure 2-2. Total utility before the introduction of money is equal to $U(a_0)$ and is entirely defined by the flow of absorption which in equilibrium is equal to the flow of income. The marginal utility of present absorption is denoted by $U'_a\,(a_0)$. It is assumed to remain unaffected by the change in real balances and is, consequently, drawn as a horizontal line.

The introduction of money yields a flow of services which, by the above assumptions, increases utility at a declining rate. For the given income/absorption a_0 the increase in overall utility is depicted by the $U(a_0,m)$ line in figure 2-2.

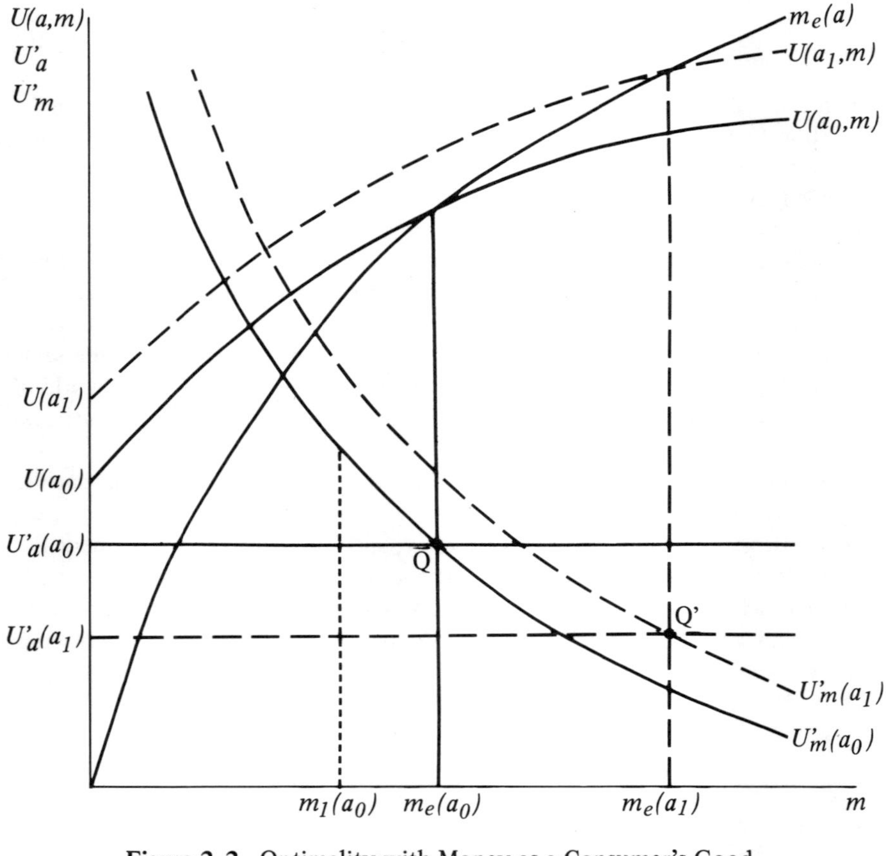

Figure 2-2. Optimality with Money as a Consumer's Good.

If money is produced at no cost and allocated freely to the residents of the country, the supply of money will be readily absorbed by residents as long as its marginal utility exceeds the marginal utility of current absorption. However, as the money supply is extended beyond point Q, the marginal utility of money falls short of the marginal utility of present absorption. Residents will, hence, substitute commodities for money. As output is fixed, this behavior will result in a rise in the general price level and, consequently, real balances will be reduced again. The pressure on prices will exist until the marginal utilities are equalized at the equilibrium level of real balances $m_e\ (a_0)$.

The above analysis indicates that, if money is treated as a consumer's good, the desired level of real balances is determined by the equality of the marginal utilities of absorption and real balances. In the long run the level of absorption, in turn, and thus the marginal utility of absorption are determined by real income. Hence, as in the case of money as a producer's good, the treatment of money as a consumer's good relates the long-run desired level of real balances uniquely to the level of real income so that equation (2.16) $l = ky$, may be equally applied to the treatment of money as a consumer's good.

It may be noted in passing that the above presentation of the role of money as a consumer's good suggests that k will not be a constant; rather it will depend upon the level of output. Generally, as output/absorption increases, the marginal utility of absorption will decline to, say, the level $U'_a\ (a_1)$ in figure 2-2 and the overall level of utility will increase to $U(a_1)$, where $a_1 > a_0$. Figure 2-2 suggests a situation in which the equilibrium level of desired real balances increases more than proportionately with the assumed increase in output/absorption. The curve relating desired real balances to alternative levels of absorption, $m_e\ (a)$ will, hence, display a convex curvature with respect to the abscissa.

The more than proportionate increase in desired real balances in response to an increase in income/absorption can be explained by reference to the theoretical reasoning about the uses of money advanced above. As output increases, the number of relative prices will grow more than proportionately and therefore, a more than proportionate increase in information is required for a rational choice. Hence the marginal utility of money (U'_m) rises alongside output. This fact is demonstrated by the shift of the U'_m line to the right. On the other hand, the marginal utility of absorption declines to $U'_a\ (a_1)$. The new equilibrium is reached at point Q′. The new desired level of real balances is given by $m_e\ (a_1)$.[27]

It is, of course, possible, and may prove to be desirable in some cases, to analyze the desired quantity of money simultaneously in its role as a producer's good and as a consumer's good.[28] Real output can then be seen to depend on the holdings of real balances by firms, whereas the liquidity services described above accrue from the holdings of real balances by households. This partition of real balances obviously does not impart the finding that desired real balances are uniquely related to a given level of real income.

The Desired Level of Real Balances in the Archibald-Lipsey Framework

The above findings about the role of money in an economy are now incorporated in the Archibald-Lipsey framework. Assume again a stationary economy with a given supply of labor, capital stock, and technology and labor productivity. Recall that the size of the capital stock is a function of the rate of time preference of the community. Initially the economy is closed. It has been demonstrated above that on the basis of these data there exists a unique level of real balances which raises output to a level at which utility from present and future consumption is maximized. This level of real balances is the level desired for the use of money as a factor of production. As it is reached this level specifies both the magnitude of permanent real income and absorption of the economy. This level is given by $y_0 = a_0$ in figure 2-3.

Recall now the arguments advanced above in the treatment of money as a consumer's good, and assume that money yields a direct utility so that for each period s the overall utility of the community is given by

$$U_s = U_s\,(a_s\,, m_s) \tag{2.20}$$

Assume furthermore that the community does not hold any money apart from that employed in the production process, and that any additional money can be obtained from the monetary authorities only at the expense of surrendering consumption goods. The community is thus faced with the choice between increasing real balances and reducing absorption.

Whereas absorption is a flow variable which yields utility in the current period only, real balances are a stock variable the utility of which is unimpaired by their use; hence, any change in their magnitude will lead to a change in permanent utility derived from them. This fact requires a multiperiod analysis of the substitution between current absorption and real balances.

The problem faced by society in period t is to maximize total lifetime utility

$$U_t = \sum_{s=0}^{\infty} U(a_{t+s}\,, m_{t+s})\frac{1}{(1+n)^s} \tag{2.21}$$

where n is the marginal rate of time preference, subject to the current period's budget constraint

$$G_t = a_t + m_t \tag{2.22}$$

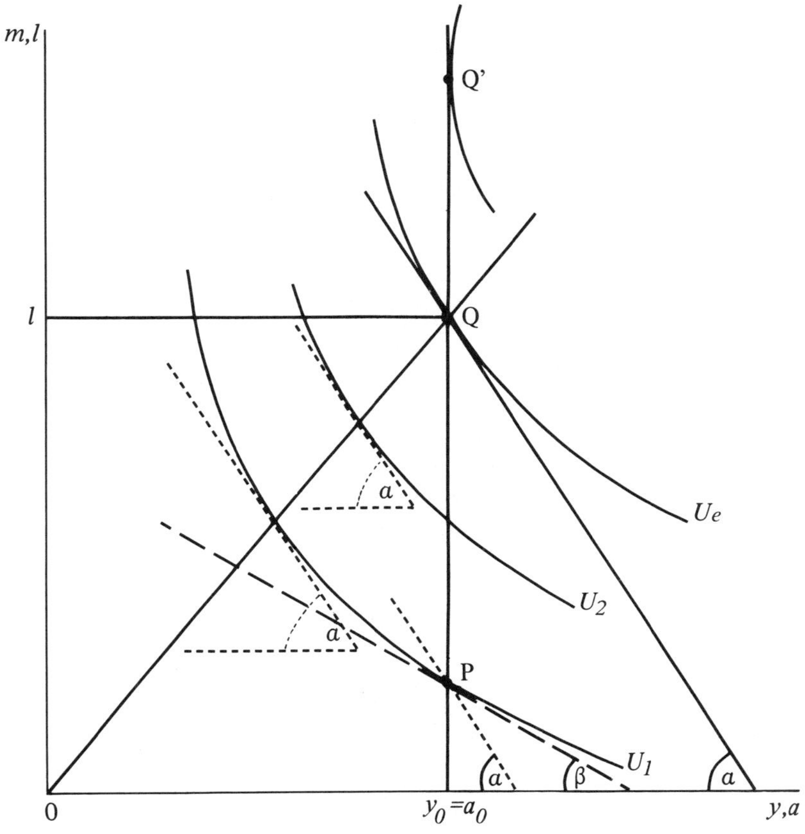

Figure 2-3. Utility Maximization with Goods and Real Balances ("Nondiscounted" Indifference Curves).

In order to arrive at the conditions for the utility-maximum form the Lagrangean function

$$V_t = \sum_{s=0}^{\infty} U(a_{t+s}, m_{t+s}) \frac{1}{(1+n)^s} + \psi(G_t - a_t - m_t) \tag{2.23}$$

This function is a modified version of the objective function (2.21) which incorporates the budget constraint. The first-order conditions for a free extremum are found by setting the partial derivates of (2.23) equal to zero

$$\frac{\delta V_t}{\delta a_t} = U_a - \psi = 0 \tag{2.23a}$$

$$\frac{\delta V_t}{\delta m_t} = U_m \sum_{s=0}^{\infty} \frac{1}{(1+n)^s} - \psi = 0 \tag{2.23b}$$

$$\frac{\delta V_t}{\delta \lambda} = G_t - a_t - m_t = 0 \tag{2.23c}$$

U_a and U_m are the partial derivatives of the utility function with respect to a and m, respectively. A comparison between equations (2.23a) and (2.23b) points to the fundamental difference between a and m, namely, the flow-versus-stock characteristics mentioned above. Equation (2.23c) automatically guarantees the satisfaction of the budget constraint. From (2.23a) and (2.23b) follows that the achievement of the constrained utility maximum requires that

$$U_a = U_m \sum_{s=0}^{\infty} \frac{1}{(1+n)^s} \tag{2.24}$$

or else that

$$\frac{U_a}{U_m} = \sum_{s=0}^{\infty} \frac{1}{(1+n)^s} \tag{2.24a}$$

where U_a/U_m is the slope of the indifference curve between current absorption and real balances.

Starting out with no money, economic agents will be prepared to acquire real balances until their marginal utility is equal to

$$U_m = \frac{U_a}{\sum_{s=0}^{\infty} \frac{1}{(1+n)^s}} \tag{2.24b}$$

In figure 2-3 the level of desired real balances l is for the given level of permanent income/absorption $y_0 = a_0$ determined at point Q. At Q the indifference curve intersects the vertical "permanent income/absorption line" with a slope

$$tg\alpha \equiv \frac{U_a}{U_m} = \sum_{s=0}^{\infty} \frac{1}{(1+n)^s}$$

The desired real-balance-to-income ratio k is given by the ray from the origin through Q.

Equation (2.24b) suggests that an inverse relationship exists between the rate of time preference and the desired level of real balances. In the extreme case of a zero rate of time preference ($n = 0$)—and assuming that $\infty < U_a < 0$—the desired level of real balances will be extended to its satiety level, i.e., to the point where the marginal utility of real balances is zero. The utility maximum will, in this case, be reached at the point of tangency between the indifference curve and the "permanent income line" at Q′.[29]

If preferences are homothetic, i.e., if the marginal rate of time preference is independent of the level of total resources, the expansion path of the system will be represented by the ray OQ. Any indifference curve in the indifference system will then display the same slope $tg\alpha = U_a/U_m$ at the point of intersection with the OQ-line. This observation implies that for the given level of permanent income y_0 a point such as P cannot be an equilibrium point since at P

$$\frac{U_a}{U_m} \equiv tg\beta < \sum_{s=0}^{\infty} \frac{1}{(1+n)^s} \equiv tg\alpha$$

Relative to the given marginal utility of absorption U_a, the marginal utility of real balances is found to be too high to bring about an equilibrium situation. The community will, therefore, be prepared to forego absorption in order to build up real balances. The rise in real balances lowers their marginal utility and thereby reduces the spread between U_a and U_m. The community will be prepared to forego absorption and build up real balances until the maximum condition, equation (2.24a), is fulfilled.

By the use of some theories about the role of money in the economy it has been possible to adapt for an economy as a whole the Archibald-Lipsey proposition that a unique and stable ratio exists between real income and desired real balances. It can be easily demonstrated that the so-determined stable long-run money demand function implies a stable long-run velocity function.

Recall that the slope of the ray through Q is equal to

$$k = \frac{m}{y} = \frac{l}{y} \tag{2.25}$$

Equation (2.25) is a modification of equation (2.16) which incorporates the assumption of equilibrium in the money market. k is the "Cambridge k," i.e., the stock of real money balances the public wants to hold as a proportion of real income. Income velocity of money is given by

$$v = \frac{y}{m} \tag{2.26}$$

so that

$$v = \frac{1}{k} \tag{2.27}$$

where both v and k are constants in the long run.

As a result of this transformation, the statement that long-run equilibrium in the economy involves a constant real-balance-to-income ratio is seen to be equivalent to the statement that the equilibrium involves a constant income velocity of money. Recall moreover that a stable long-run money-demand function is one of the centerpieces of the monetary approach to the balance of payments. This finding indicates that the Archibald-Lipsey framework is entirely compatible with the monetary approach to balance-of-payments analysis and can thus be applied as a diagrammatic device for demonstrating the adjustment processes expounded by the monetary approach.

The Dynamics of Adjustment to a Devaluation

The preceding analysis investigated the determinants of the long-run equilibrium position of an economy and established certain well specified relationships between key variables in an economy. It is now possible to introduce an exogenous shock to the system and to trace the adjustment path that the economy is likely to follow.

Assume for simplicity a stationary open economy. In the first part of the analysis the economy is "open" only in a rudimentary sense in that its economic realtions with "the rest of the world" are restricted to the exchange of goods and money. Neither the stock of capital nor property rights to it or any other domestic debt instrument are tradable. As such the analysis is restricted to the trade account, the capital account being zero by assumption. The economy operates in a system of fixed exchange rates. The economy is small in that variations in domestic economic aggregates do not affect the equilibrium position of the rest of the world. In particular the small open economy cannot affect the world price of its exports or imports. As a result, it faces given terms of trade, and exports and imports may be treated as a composite good in the Hicksian sense.

Assuming that goods arbitrage is perfect, prices cannot diverge between countries. Given the foreign currency price of the composite good, P^*, the domestic price of exportables and importables, P, is given by

$$P = e \times P^* \tag{2.28}$$

where e is the exchange rate, i.e., the price of foreign in terms of domestic currency. Assuming that all goods produced domestically are tradable, equation (2.28) represents the relation between the domestic and the foreign price level. Equation (2.28) also indicates that in the absence of exchange-rate changes the domestic price level is invariably given for the small open economy.

The economy is assumed to be in full stock-and-flow equilibrium at the beginning. Figure 2-4 describes this state in diagrammatic form. As in figure 2-3,

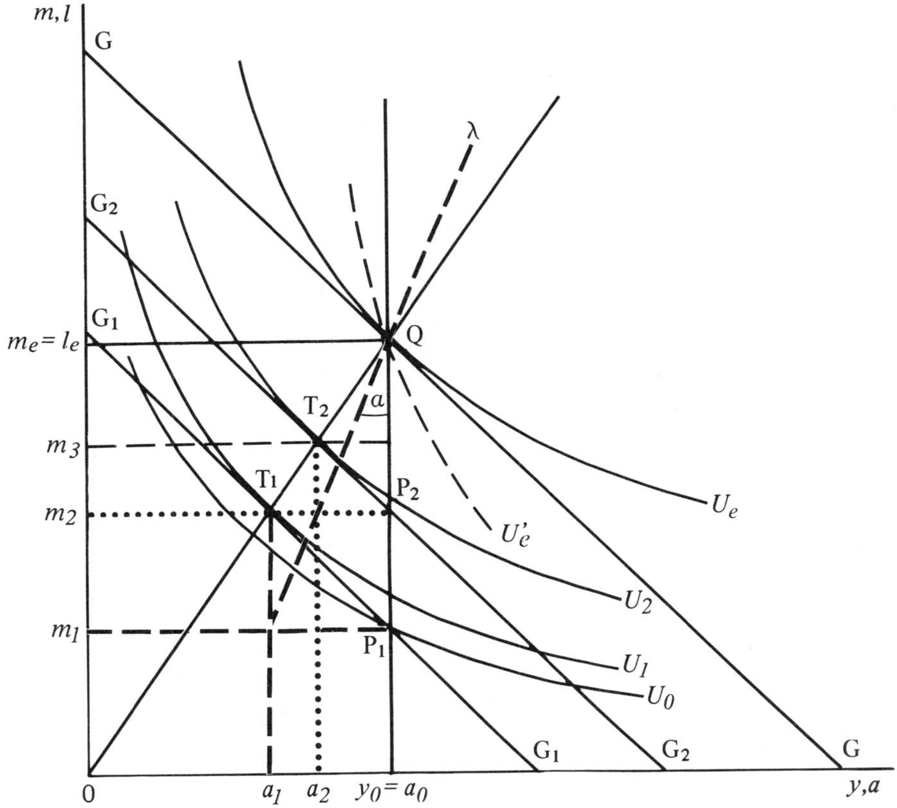

Figure 2-4. Adjustment Process after a Devaluation ("Discounted Indifference Curves").

the abscissa denotes both the quantity of goods produced domestically (real income) and real domestic absorption. The ordinate measures actual and desired real balances, m and l, respectively.

At a point in time $t = 0$, total resources (G) consist of y_0 units of real income, recurrently produced from period to period, and m_e units of real balances. Total resources determine the choices between absorption and holding real balances open to the economy. In figure 2-4 these choices are represented by the GG line through Q. The budget line, which relates domestic goods to real balances, has an invariant slope of 135°. This reflects the fact that the small country, when absorbing more or less than it produces, does not exercise any influence on the world price of commodities. As a result, real balances can be converted into real absorption (and vice versa) at a fixed one-to-one rate, i.e., $dm = -da$.

Initial full stock-and-flow equilibrium is represented by point Q. At Q the first-order conditions (2.23a–2.23c) are assumed to be fulfilled. Real absorption is equal to real income and actual real balances m_e are equal to their long-run desired level l_e. As a result of this the balance of payments is zero. Point Q in figure 2-4 corresponds to point Q in figure 2-3. Figure 2-4 displays, however, a modification in the shape and, thus, in the interpretation of the indifference system. The modification has been introduced in order to enhance the clarity of the diagrammatic presentation. By the small-country assumption, the relationship between changes in real balances and absorption is invariably constrained to be equal to minus one ($dm/da = -1$).

As observed above, this fact determines the slope of the budget line GG. Furthermore, equations (2.21) to (2.24b) imply that the constrained maximization of lifetime utility requires for each period that

$$-\frac{dm}{da} = \frac{U_a}{U_m \sum_{s=0}^{\infty} \frac{1}{(1+n)^s}} \tag{2.29}$$

Lifetime utility is, hence, maximized at the point of tangency between the budget line and the indifference curve for current absorption and the *discounted* (over lifetime) value of real balances. The modified indifference system in Figure 2-4 expresses this latter relation, whereas the system in figure 2-3 depicts the relation between the *undiscounted* single-period relative marginal utilities.[30] The change in the meaning of the indifference system and the corresponding adjustment in the diagrammatic presentation allow for an immediate and straightforward determination of the utility-maximizing combination of absorption and real balances for each level of total resources.

Consider now the case of a devaluation of the home country's currency.

Given the foreign currency price of all commodities and assuming that goods arbitrage is perfect and instantaneous, a devaluation will lead to an immediate, equiproportionate increase in domestic prices.[31]

$$\hat{P} = \hat{e} \tag{2.30}$$

where a circumflex superimposed over a variable indicates a percentage change, e.g.,

$$\hat{e} = \frac{1}{e}\frac{de}{dt} \tag{2.31}$$

At the initial level of nominal money balances, a rise in the domestic price level leads to a decline in real balances by the same percentage[32]

$$\hat{m} = -\hat{e} \tag{2.32}$$

In figure 2-4 this cut in real-money balances is represented by the decline of M/P from m_e to m_1. Total resources of the economy consist now of y_0 units of real income and m_1 units of real balances. The new set of choices between absorption and real balances open to the economy is given by the G_1G_1 line through P_1. If economic agents decide to maintain the old level of absorption, society will enjoy a level of utility marked by the indifference curve U_0. It is immediately obvious from figure 2-4, however, that this type of behavior is not to be expected because it leads to a suboptimal level of utility. At point P_1 the indifference curve U_0 intersects the new budget line G_1G_1 from below, indicating that for the exogenously given exchange ratio between absorption and real balances the marginal utility of the latter is too high relative to that of the former. This observation implies an excess demand for money and an equal excess supply of goods. Equations (2.24-2.24b) suggest that the exact size of the excess demand (supply) depends on the marginal rate of time preference as well as on the size of the reduction in m which translates into the change in its marginal utility.

The impact effect of a change in the exchange rate on the desired levels of a and m can be evaluated more rigorously by the use of matrix algebra in the analysis of constrained utility maximization. Recall equations (2.23a-2.30). Total differentiation of these equations and expression of the result in matrix form yields

$$\begin{bmatrix} U_{aa} & U_{am}DF & -1 \\ U_{ma}DF & U_{mm}DF & -1 \\ -1 & -1 & 0 \end{bmatrix} \begin{bmatrix} da \\ dm \\ d\psi \end{bmatrix} = \begin{bmatrix} 0 \\ 0 \\ -dG \end{bmatrix}$$

Matrix 2.1

where the U_{ii}'s and U_{ij}'s are the second derivatives of the utility function with respect to the home country (i) and the foreign (j) arguments. The U_{ii}'s are generally negative, and the U_{ij}'s are greater than or equal to zero.[33] Furthermore, it holds that $U_{ij} = U_{ji}$. For simplicity the subscripts indicating the time period have been omitted in the presentation. The coefficient matrix for the second derivatives of equation (2.23) is the endogenous variable Jacobian $|J|$ which, in turn, is identical with the bordered Hessian $|\bar{H}|$.[34]

The impact effect of a change in the exchange rate is found by dividing the total differentials through by de. The matrix then takes the form of

$$|J| \times \begin{bmatrix} da/de \\ dm/de \\ d\psi/de \end{bmatrix} = \begin{bmatrix} 0 \\ 0 \\ -dG/de \end{bmatrix}$$

Matrix 2.2

Since $m = M/eP^*$ it follows from (2.22) that $dG/de = -m$.[35] Making use of Cramer's rule, matrix 2.2 can be solved for the three comparative-static derivatives, da/de, dm/de and $d\lambda/de$, of which $d\lambda/de$ can be neglected here

$$\frac{da}{de} = \frac{1}{|J|} \begin{bmatrix} 0 & U_{am}DF & -1 \\ 0 & U_{mm}DF & -1 \\ m & -1 & 0 \end{bmatrix} = \frac{m}{|J|} \begin{bmatrix} U_{am}DF & -1 \\ U_{mm}DF & -1 \end{bmatrix} \qquad (2.33)$$

$$\frac{dm}{de} = \frac{1}{|J|} \begin{bmatrix} U_{aa} & 0 & -1 \\ U_{ma}DF & 0 & -1 \\ -1 & m & 0 \end{bmatrix} = \frac{-m}{|J|} \begin{bmatrix} U_{aa} & -1 \\ U_{mm}DF & -1 \end{bmatrix} \qquad (2.34)$$

or alternatively

$$\frac{da}{de} = \frac{m\,|C_{31}|}{|J|} < 0 \qquad (2.33a)$$

$$\frac{dm}{de} = \frac{m\,|C_{32}|}{|J|} < 0 \qquad (2.34a)$$

where the $|C_{ij}|$'s are the cofactors of the respective row elements in the above three-by-three matrices. The second-order condition for a maximum requires that the bordered Hessian $|\bar{H}| = |J|$ is positive. Solving the above determinant this is found to be true. $|C_{31}|$ and $|C_{32}|$, on the other hand, are negative. The excess demand for goods (EDG) is given by

$$EDG = a - y \tag{2.35}$$

and consequently

$$\frac{dEDG}{de} = \frac{da}{de} - \frac{dy}{de} \tag{2.35a}$$

Since dy/de is zero by assumption and da/de is negative, utility-maximizing behavior implies an excess supply of goods of the size $m|C_{31}|/|J|$ for the first period. A similar calculation for the money market yields[36]

$$\frac{dEDM}{de} = \frac{m|C_{32}|}{|J|} + m > 0^{37} \tag{2.36}$$

where EDM is the excess demand for real balances. By substituting (2.33a) into (2.35a) and by a simple transformation of the so-modified equation (2.35a) as well as of equation (2.36) it can be shown that the utility-maximizing excess supply of goods is equal to the excess demand for real balances. For a given change in the exchange rate, the excess demand for real balances (excess supply of goods) is larger, the smaller the initial level of real balances, m, and the smaller the marginal rate of time preference, n (i.e., the larger DF). It will also be larger, the larger U_{mm} and U_{am} and the smaller U_{aa} and U_{ma}. The latter factors determine the curvature of the indifference system.

In figure 2-4 the equilibrium position for the first period is given by the point of tangency (T_1) between an indifference curve and the budget line G_1G_1. Given homothetic preferences, the point of tangency must lie on the income velocity line OQ. In the first period after the devaluation, the utility-maximizing level of absorption will consequently decline to a_1. The small-country assumption now ensures two not unrelated results. First, the elasticity of foreign demand for domestic goods is infinite so that the excess supply of goods of the home country is fully absorbed by the rest of the world. Second, the excess supply of domestic goods does not alter the world price level. Both taken together bring about a balance-of-payments (or more exact, balance-of-trade) surplus, the real value of which is equal to the decline in real absorption, $a_0 - a_1$; this surplus raises real balances by an equal amount, i.e., by $m_2 - m_1$.

In the next period the country starts with an unchanged income of y_0 and a level of real balances m_2. The new budget line is given by G_2G_2 through P_2. Utility maximization requires again that absorption fall short of income. As a result of the decline in the marginal utility of real balances brought about by their increase in the first period, the shortfall in spending will, however, be smaller in this period than in the first period, as is witnessed by the equilibrium point for period two, T_2. As absorption a_2 again falls short of income, a further trade-account surplus of $y_0 - a_2$ will accrue and lead to an increase in real balances by $m_3 - m_2$. This process will continue until actual real balances return to their desired level at point Q. Real absorption will be equal to real income again and the balance of payments will be zero.

The dynamics of the adjustment and the conditions for the stability of the desired real-balance-to-income ratio can be most conveniently and more rigorously demonstrated by the use of differential calculus.

Recall equations

$$B = dR/dt \tag{2.1}$$

$$dM/dt = dR/dt \text{[38]} \tag{2.5}$$

$$B/P \equiv dR/Pdt = y - a \tag{2.7}$$

$$a = y + \lambda(M/P - L/P) \tag{2.8}$$

Since $M/P \equiv m$ and $L/P \equiv l$ and by (2.16), $l = ky$, equation (2.8) can be rewritten as

$$a = y + \lambda(m - ky) \tag{2.8a}$$

Equation (2.8a) summarizes in a simple and comprehensive way the utility-maximizing choice between absorption and real balances, as described above. Differentiation of (2.8a) with respect to m yields $da/dm = \lambda$. Assuming that (2.8a) reflects rational behavior in spending of economic agents, the absorption-velocity coefficient λ[39] is thus seen to represent the utility-maximizing change in absorption in the event of an exogenous change in real balances. In particular, λ is seen to depend on the marginal rate of time preference, $\lambda = \lambda(n)$.[40]

Substitution of (2.5) into (2.1) and subsequently (2.1) into (2.7) yields

$$\frac{dM}{dt}\frac{1}{P} = y - a \tag{2.37}$$

Substitution of (2.8a) into (2.37), multiplication by P, and rearranging of items yields

$$\frac{dM}{dt} + \lambda M = \lambda\, k\, y\, P \tag{2.38}$$

The special attention given in this study to the effects of exchange-rate changes is enhanced by choosing a foreign price level equal to unity [P* = 1 in equation (2.28)] so that the domestic price level equals the exchange rate, $P = e$. Hence, equation (2.38) can be rewritten as follows:

$$\frac{dM}{dt} + \lambda M = \lambda\, k\, y\, e \tag{2.38a}$$

The general solution of this nonhomogeneous differential equation is given by

$$M(t) = A\bar{e}^{-\lambda t} + k\, y\, e_1 \tag{2.39}$$

where A is an arbitrary constant and $\bar{e}$ is the natural exponential function, which is not to be confused with e, the exchange rate. Solving for A in the case of $t = 0$ and substituting the result into (2.35) yields

$$M(t) = k\, y\, (e_0 - e_1)\, \bar{e}^{-\lambda t} + k\, y\, e_1 \tag{2.39a}$$

Equation (2.39a) describes the adjustment process following a change in the exchange rate. A devaluation ($e_1 > e_0$) leads to a continuous asymptotic increase in the money supply and, given the new domestic price level, in real money balances. The process continues until the new equilibrium level of money balances

$$M_e = k\, y\, e_1 = k\, y\, P_1 \tag{2.40}$$

is reached. Money balances will have increased by the same percentage as the exchange rate and the domestic price level; real balances will be back at their former level and, thus, be equal again to their desired level. The path of adjustment of the nominal money supply is depicted in figure 2-5a. The adjustment path of the balance of payments is derived in the following way. From equations (2.1) and (2.5) follows that $B = dM(t)/dt$; therefore by equation 2.39a

$$B = -\lambda\, k\, y\, (e_0 - e_1)\, \bar{e}^{-\lambda t} \tag{2.41}$$

The path of adjustment of the balance of payments[41] is depicted in figure 2-5b. The first-period change in the balance of payments is equal to $-\lambda\, k\, y\, (e_0 - e_1)$. As time goes by the size of the balance-of-payments surpluses converges asymptotically toward zero.

Equations (2.39a) and (2.41) allow for an investigation into the stability of the adjustment process after a devaluation. Equation (2.39a) shows that the money supply will converge to its new equilibrium value $M_e = k\, y\, P_1$ as long as absorption velocity λ is greater than zero and smaller than unity.[42] Only if a difference between actual and desired real-money balances does not matter for real behavior, i.e., if $\lambda = 0$, will there be no automatic adjustment in response to a change in the exchange rate within this model.[43]

A complement to the finding that the nominal money supply converges to a new equilibrium value is the fact that the balance of payments converges to zero.

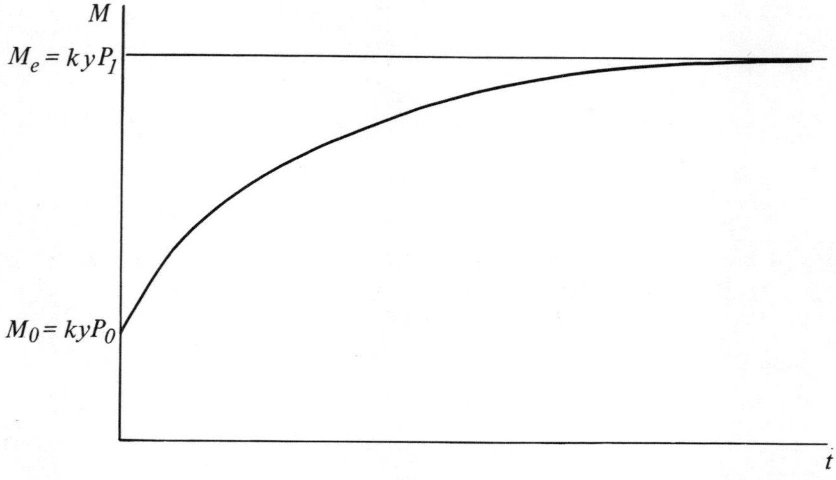

Figure 2-5a. Adjustment of Money Supply after a Devaluation.

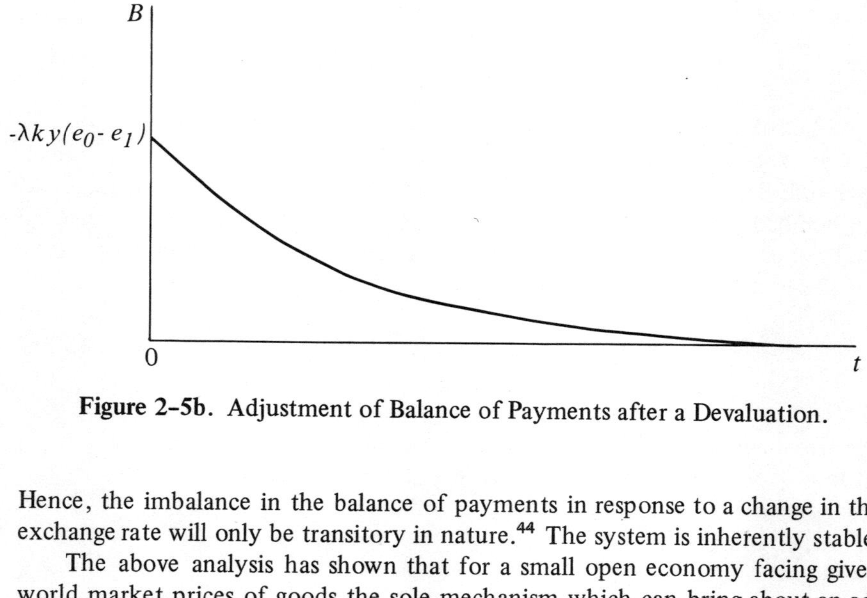

Figure 2-5b. Adjustment of Balance of Payments after a Devaluation.

Hence, the imbalance in the balance of payments in response to a change in the exchange rate will only be transitory in nature.[44] The system is inherently stable.

The above analysis has shown that for a small open economy facing given world market prices of goods the sole mechanism which can bring about an adjustment toward equilibrium in response to a change in the exchange rate is a variation in the domestic money supply via a change in the foreign component of the monetary base. This change in the foreign component of the monetary base is brought about by a temporary act of saving by domestic residents, which frees part of domestic production for exportation.

For a large country there are essentially two ways of bringing about adjustment. The first is again a change in the domestic money supply via balance-of-payments surpluses or deficits. The second is a variation in the domestic and in the world price level in response to the adjustment in spending. The change in the price level will affect the value of actual real balances and, thereby, contribute to an equalization of actual and desired real balances, which is the prerequisite for a stable equilibrium.[45]

The Application of an Enlarged Wealth Concept: Nontraded Bonds

Presentation of the Concept

The analysis thus far has focused on the bare essentials of a model which could describe the process of adjustment after an exogenous disturbance in a monetary economy. Some of the assumptions made above are unduly restrictive and may be removed now that the essentials of the system have been presented.

A major restriction in the foregoing analysis has been the assumption that money is the only asset which enters the utility function of economic agents. Another asset, the capital stock, exists but is treated separately from utility-maximization considerations. In the modified Archibald-Lipsey framework, its size is considered predetermined, and its importance derives solely from its influence on real income of the economy. This dichotomy prevents an all-embracing view of the utility-maximizing choices open to a monetary economy and bars the analysis of a number of interesting short-run adjustment processes resulting from exchange-rate changes.

In the analysis of money as a producer's good, allusion was made to the fact that the equilibrium capital stock is a function of the rate of time preference. This demonstrates that the equilibrium capital stock is subject to utility-maximization considerations. More specifically, the equilibrium capital stock is determined by utility maximization over time. People derive utility not from the capital stock per se but from the output it produces in current and in future periods.

Present-period absorption can be increased by selling part or all of the capital stock. The cost involved in this transaction is a loss in real income, and thus in equilibrium absorption, a loss over all future periods. The true trade-off is therefore between present and future absorption. To the extent that a given and constant relation exists between the capital stock and output, the capital stock can be introduced directly into the utility function. As the capital stock is added as another component into the utility function, it also becomes part of the desired level of wealth. Furthermore, it enters explicitly the budget constraint of the economy. Measured in terms of consumption goods, the value of the capital stock is given by

$$b = \frac{P_k K}{P} \tag{2.42}$$

where P_k is the market price per unit of capital, and b can also be interpreted as the real value of property rights to the capital stock or as the real value of bonds.

The utility-maximization problem presented in the previous chapters is modified in the following way: At any point in time, t, society attempts to maximize lifetime utility

$$U_t = \sum_{s=0}^{\infty} U(a_{t+s}, b_{t+s}, m_{t+s}) \frac{1}{(1+n)^s} \tag{2.43}$$

subject to the budget constraint

$$G_t = y_t + P_{k_t} K_t / P_t + M_t / P_t \tag{2.44}$$

or else given that $a_t = y_t$ initially

$$G_t = a_t + b_t + m_t \tag{2.44a}$$

Differentiation of the Lagrangean function

$$V_t = \sum_{s=0}^{\infty} U(a_{t+s}, b_{t+s}, m_{t+s}) + \psi(G_t - a_t - b_t - m_t) \tag{2.45}$$

yields the first-order condition for a free extremum

$$V_a = U_a - \psi = 0 \tag{2.45a}$$

$$V_b = U_b DF - \psi = 0 \tag{2.45b}$$

$$V_m = U_m DF - \psi = 0 \tag{2.45c}$$

$$V_\psi = G_t - a_t - b_t - m_t = 0 \tag{2.45d}$$

where the V_i's are the first derivatives of equation (2.45) with respect to the argument i. Equation (2.45d) guarantees the satisfaction of the wealth constraint.

For an extremum it is necessary that

$$\psi = U_a = U_b DF = U_m DF \tag{2.46}$$

or alternatively that

$$U_a = U_b DF \tag{2.46a}$$

$$U_a = U_m DF \tag{2.46b}$$

$$U_b = U_m \tag{2.46c}$$

where DF is, as in the previous section, the discount factor, $\Sigma_{s=0}^{\infty} 1/(1 + n)^s$.

The first-order conditions thus imply for the full equilibrium a unique absorption-to-real-bonds, absorption-to-real-balance, and real-balance-to-real-bonds ratio. Rather than possessing a desired real-balance-to-real-income ratio, as has been suggested in the previous sections, the economy is thus seen to possess a desired real-wealth-to-real-income ratio where wealth consists of both the real value of bonds and real balances ($w = b + m$).

In figure 2-6 this ratio is depicted by the ray from the origin 0 through Q. Q is the only point at which the condition for utility maximization

$$U_a = U_w DF \text{ or } U_a/U_w DF = 1$$

is fulfilled.[46] Graphically, this is represented by the fact that the discounted version[47] of the indifference curve U_0 is tangential to the budget constraint GG at point Q. The panel to the right of the income line y_0Q describes the equilibrium allocation of wealth between real bonds and real balances, PE_0. In equilibrium the economy holds RQ = RS_0 units of real bonds and y_0R = AS_0 = AG units of real balances.

The Effects of a Devaluation

Assume again a devaluation of the home country's currency. Assume furthermore that even after the introduction of domestic bonds the only items exchanged internationally are goods and money: neither domestic nor foreign bonds are tradable internationally. This restriction, which is abandoned in the next section, highlights a number of interesting adjustment processes and interdependencies which cannot be easily demonstrated in a model which assumes perfect capital mobility.

The impact of a devaluation on first-period desired real absorption, bonds,

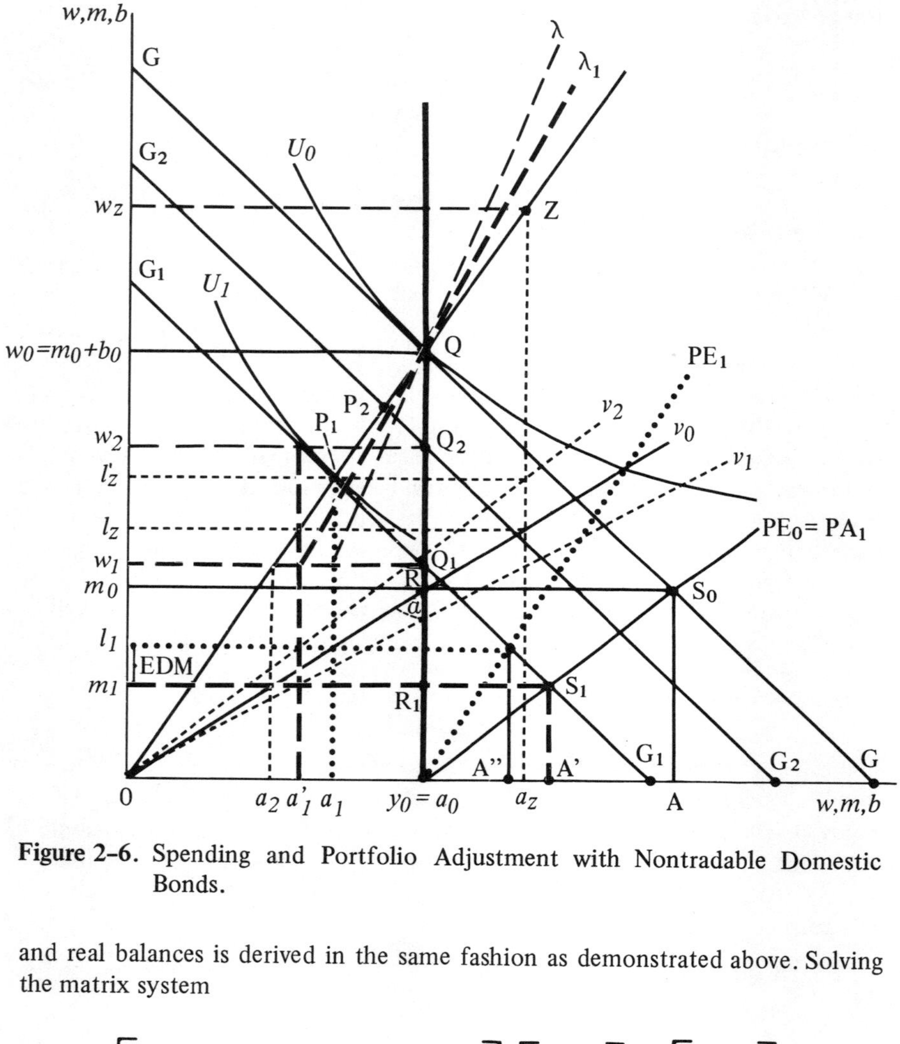

Figure 2-6. Spending and Portfolio Adjustment with Nontradable Domestic Bonds.

and real balances is derived in the same fashion as demonstrated above. Solving the matrix system

$$\begin{bmatrix} U_{aa} & U_{ab} & U_{am} & -1 \\ U_{ba}DF & U_{bb}DF & U_{bm}DF & -1 \\ U_{ma}DF & U_{mb}DF & U_{mm}DF & -1 \\ -1 & -1 & -1 & 0 \end{bmatrix} \begin{bmatrix} da/de \\ db/de \\ dm/de \\ d\psi/de \end{bmatrix} = \begin{bmatrix} 0 \\ 0 \\ 0 \\ -dG/de \end{bmatrix}$$

Matrix 2.3

for *a*, *b*, and *m* yields[48]

$$\frac{da}{de} = \frac{(b + m)\ |C_{41}|}{|J|} \tag{2.47}$$

$$\frac{db}{de} = \frac{(b + m)\ |C_{42}|}{|J|} \tag{2.48}$$

$$\frac{dm}{de} = \frac{(b + m)\ |C_{43}|}{|J|} \tag{2.49}$$

$|J|$ is negative, as required by the second-order condition for a maximum. $|C_{41}|$ is positive, hence da/de is negative, indicating that there will be an excess supply of goods. Both $|C_{42}|$ and $|C_{43}|$ are also positive; hence, both the demand for bonds and real balances will decline. This decline is, however, smaller than the devaluation-induced change in the real value of bonds and money. As a result, the economy will experience an excess demand for both real bonds and real balances.[49]

In figure 2-6 the effects of a devaluation are demonstrated in graphic form. The devaluation-induced rise in the domestic price level lowers the real value of both money and bonds and, thus, total wealth. The new real value of wealth w_1 is given by point Q_1, real balances are reduced to m_1 (point R_1) and the value of real bonds is equal to $w_1 - m_1 = Q_1 - R_1$. The first-period budget constraint is depicted by the G_1G_1 line through Q_1. Utility-maximizing absorption is determined by the point of tangency between the indifference curve U_1 and this budget constraint. Ceteris paribus this point of tangency has to lie at the intersection of the expansion path OQ with the budget line, i.e., at point P_1. Desired absorption is given by a_1. Absorption velocity $\lambda = da/dw$ which reflects fully the utility-maximizing decision-making processes incorporated in equation (2.47) is given by the λ-line through Q. At the given level of the income velocity of money ($v_0 = tg\alpha$), the economy requires l_1 units of real balances to finance the desired level of absorption a_1. The actual level of real balances m_1 lies, however, well below the level required to finance desired current transactions. Although after the devaluation the actual allocation of wealth $y_0Q_1 = y_0G_1$ between real bonds and real balances is still given by $PE_0 = PA_1$ with $y_0A' = Q_1R_1$ units of b and $A'S_1 = A'G_1$ units of m, the desired allocation is denoted by the y_0PE_1 ray with y_0A'' units of bonds and $A''G_1$ units of real balances. Economic agents will, therefore, attempt to sell off bonds. By assumption, neither are domestic debt instruments internationally tradable nor do domestic residents hold foreign financial assets that they could sell off in exchange for the required money balances. Therefore, the aggregate attempt of residents to sell off bonds will force their price down and their interest rate up.

The rise in the return on bonds will induce two distinct adjustments on the part of economic agents. The first concerns the intertemporal distribution of absorption. The second affects the desired allocation of wealth between money and bonds.

The rise in the interest rate disturbs the initial equality between the internal rate of time preference and the interest rate and makes it more "profitable" to forego utility derived from present absorption in order to raise future utility, which stems from both increased future absorption and increased services of real balances. As the interest rate rises, absorption velocity increases, as shown by its new line λ_1, thereby reducing desired absorption to a_1'.

A second, simultaneous effect of the rise in the interest rate is that it induces people to make more efficient use of existing money balances. In figure 2-6 this behavior is reflected in a higher income velocity of circulation, ν_1. The adjustment in the interest rate continues until the desired level of current absorption and the income velocity have adjusted such that the financing requirements for that level of absorption are met by the existing money stock, i.e., until equilibrium in the money market is obtained. This situation is reached at a level of absorption of a_1' which, given the higher income velocity ν_1, can be fully financed by the existing money stock m_1. In the first period the country will experience a balance-of-payments surplus equal to $y_0 - a_1' = Q_2Q_1$ in real terms. In the next period the country will start out from a level of total resources indicated by the G_2G_2 line. Again spending will fall short of income, and the country will accumulate another, though smaller, balance-of-payments surplus. Eventually, full equilibrium will be reestablished at Q.[50]

In the initial model, in which economic agents possessed only one financial asset and which did not allow for interest-rate effects, the entire burden of adjustment was borne by an adjustment in spending which resulted in a change in the level of utility derived from absorption; this tended to alleviate the loss in utility from reduced real balances after the devaluation. In the present case, the existence of a second financial asset and the related interest-rate effects entail a simultaneous adjustment in the demand for money on top of the adjustment in the demand for goods. The decline in the demand for money induced by the rise in the interest rate finds its expression in an increase in the velocity of circulation of existing money balances. This increase reduces the convenience yield of real balances below the level experienced before the devaluation. Utility maximization for each period involves the equalization of the marginal utilities of present absorption, future absorption (represented by the real value of bonds), and the convenience yield of real balances. The adjustment processes described in this section are a reflection of these utility-maximizing choices made by the economic agents of the devaluating country.

The presentation has highlighted the fact that in the event of a change in the exchange rate the existence of an additional (interest-bearing) financial asset tends to mitigate the initial shock in the goods and money markets. Part of the adjustment is now transferred to the equilibrating forces operating in the markets of financial assets, notably the interest rate. In the absence of the interest effect on income velocity v, the level of absorption would have had to decline to a_2, the interest-rate-induced rise in the income velocity of money lowers the first-period equilibrium decline in absorption to a_1'.

The Application of an Enlarged Wealth Concept: Traded Bonds

Adjustments in the Basic Framework

A major restriction in the analysis of exchange-rate changes that exists even after the modifications introduced in the preceding chapter is the assumption that the international economic relations of the home country are restricted to the exchange of goods and money so that capital movements are excluded. The abandonment of this assumption requires a number of adjustments in the basic model and in the technique of handling the Archibald-Lipsey diagram. This section will present the fundamental adjustments in a model which incorporates internationally traded bonds. The understanding of the adjustment process in response to a change in the exchange rate will be facilitated by this presentation.

The intention of the previous section was to highlight the interest rate effects on the adjustment process after a devaluation. For demonstration purposes, trade in financial assets and the accompanying mitigating influence of international capital flows on the domestic interest rate were, therefore, excluded. In this section a diametrically opposite position is taken. Bonds, both domestic and foreign, become internationally tradable and are considered perfect substitutes by residents of both countries. Without loss of generality it is assumed that the foreign rate of return exceeds the domestic rate, i.e., $r^* > r$.[51]

A number of adjustments follow from these assumptions. First, the higher rate of interest abroad raises the level of wealth desired by domestic residents. The motive for this increase in desired wealth lies in the newly generated disequilibrium between the (foreign) interest rate and the marginal rate of time preference; by a temporary act of saving domestic residents can acquire property rights to foreign capital which yield a permanent stream of interest payments higher than the one yielded by domestic capital. By acquiring foreign capital, domestic residents can thus raise the flow of permanent income and utility and, thereby, equilibrate the marginal rate of time preference and the interest rate. The small-country assumption implies that the price of foreign capital remains unaffected by this operation, so that the rate of return on property rights to foreign capital is constant over time.

Given free and frictionless trade in bonds, perfect capital mobility, and perfect substitutability between domestic and foreign bonds, the price of a unit of domestic capital cannot deviate from the price of a unit of foreign capital. Thus, the second type of adjustment relates to the value of the physical stock of capital (which remains unchanged by assumption) in terms of consumption goods. The higher rate of return abroad implies a lower relative price of capital abroad than at home: $P_k^* < P_k$, where P_k^* is the foreign price of capital. As trade in bonds is opened, domestic residents will substitute foreign for domestic bonds; consequently, the price of domestic capital (bonds) and thereby the value of bonds in terms of consumption goods falls, whereas the rate of return on domestic capital rises to the international level.

A third type of adjustment concerns the desired level of real balances. As the rate of return on capital rises, the opportunity costs of holding money increase. Individuals will, therefore, substitute domestic and foreign capital for real balances until the marginal utilities of the two forms of wealth are equal. The result of this substitution is a permanent increase in the income velocity of money circulation.

These adjustments will, finally, affect the long-run equilibrium levels of income and absorption. The acquisition of foreign interest- earning assets will lead to a permanent stream of interest payments from abroad to domestic residents and, thereby, raise both the level of domestic real disposable income and absorption.

Figure 2-7 illustrates the effects of the adjustments described above. The initial equilibrium wealth-to-income ratio is depicted by the ray $(\bar{w}/y)_0$ in the right-hand panel of figure 2-7. Wealth consists of r_0P units of real balances and PR units of domestic bonds (capital). Initial income velocity is given by the ray $r_0 v_0$. The left-hand panel indicates, first, the desired level of wealth as a function of the domestic and foreign interest rates, $\bar{w}$ $(r, \bar{r}^*)$. As either rate increases beyond the initial equilibrium level r_0 (depicted at the origin) so does the desired level of wealth. Second, it describes the negative relation between the desired level of real balances and the interest rate, $l(r)$. Stated differently, it describes the positive relation between the velocity of circulation and the interest rate. And third, it depicts the change in the real value of a given stock of capital in terms of consumption goods as the interest rate rises (the price of capital declines). As r rises, $b(r)$ approaches $l(r)$ asymptotically. Given a world interest rate of r^*, the new equilibrium situation after the opening of trade in bonds is characterized by a higher desired-wealth-to-income ratio, $(\bar{w}/y)_1$; a lower level of desired real balances, r_0P′; a lower real value of domestic capital, P′R′, and a newly acquired stock of foreign bonds R′S. The rise in the income velocity of circulation accompanying the rise in the domestic interest rate is indicated in the right-hand panel by the downward shift of the v_0 ray to v_1.

Real wealth of the domestic economy consists now of three components: real balances, m, the real value of domestic bonds, b, and the real value of domestically owned foreign bonds, b^*. All three assets are measured in terms of consumption goods, and the latter is expressed in domestic currency, i.e., $b^* = eB^*/P$. B^* is hence the nominal foreign currency value of foreign bonds

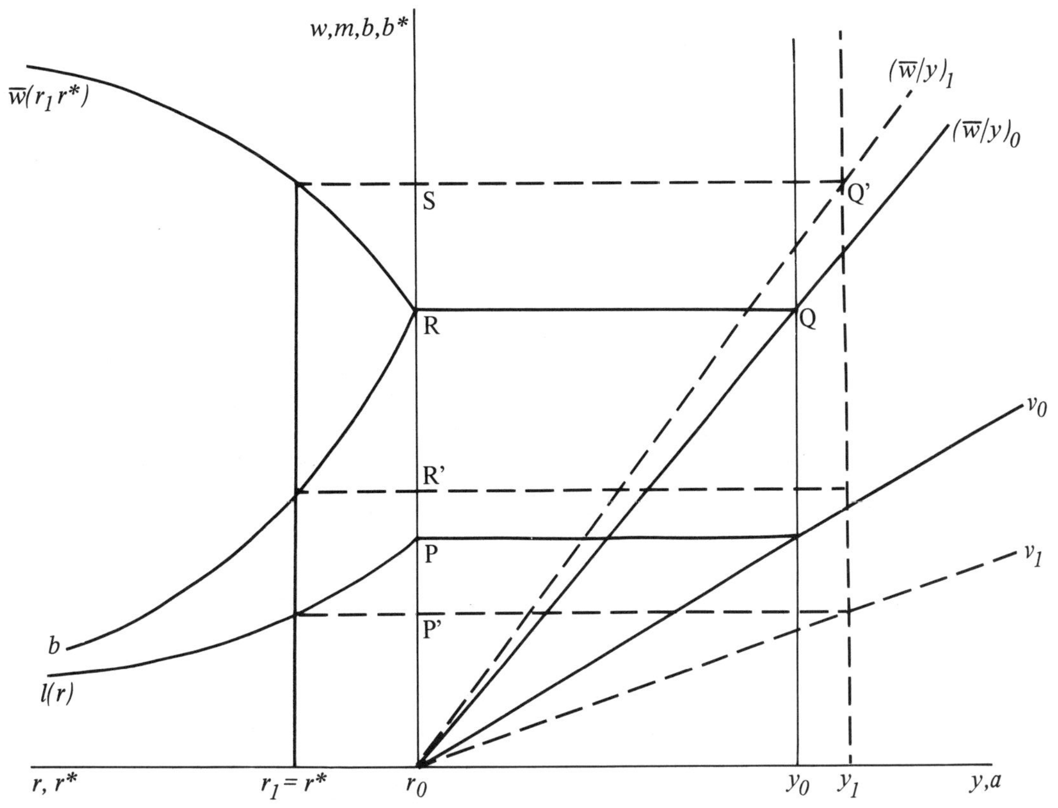

Figure 2-7. Adjustments in the Domestic Economy after the Introduction of Internationally Tradable Bonds.

held by domestic residents. Total real wealth in domestic currency after trade in bonds is opened is then given by

$$w = \frac{M + B + eB^*}{P} \equiv m + b + b^* \tag{2.50}$$

where $B = P_k K$. In figure 2-7 this level of total real wealth is measured by the distance r_0S or y_1Q′.

Interest payments on domestically owned foreign bonds raise disposable income to y_1. Domestically produced income is denoted by y_0, and the real value of foreign interest payments equals $y_1 - y_0$. Real disposable income of the economy is, therefore, given by

$$y^d = y_0 + r^*eB^*/P \tag{2.51}$$

where the latter part of the sum represents the real value of interest payments. These interest payments lead to a service-account surplus which is matched by a deficit of equal size in the trade account. In figure 2-7, $y_1 - y_0$ therefore expresses both the full equilibrium size of the service-account surplus and the trade-account deficit in real terms.

The Effects of a Devaluation

Consider now a devaluation of the home country's currency in a system that allows for trade both in goods and in bonds.

The small-country assumption, when applied in connection with the assumption of perfect capital mobility, ensures that during the entire process of adjustment the domestic interest rate is equal to the foreign interest rate, which is assumed to be constant. This assumption facilitates the technique of the diagrammatic exposition of the adjustment process; at the same time it puts special emphasis on the role of capital flows in the adjustment process. The preceding analysis has demonstrated that, with an unchanged rate of interest, the desired level of wealth will remain unchanged during the entire process of adjustment. By the same token the income velocity of circulation of money will not vary during the adjustment process. In other words, demand for real balances will be a constant fraction of real income (output) if money is considered a producer's good and a constant fraction of real absorption if money is considered a consumer's good. Assume that money fulfills both roles and that the supply of money for production is not affected by the devaluation so that real output remains at its initial level.

The impact of a devaluation on absorption and the demand for domestic and foreign bonds as well as for money is again demonstrated by the use of matrix algebra. Considering that, after the inclusion of foreign bonds, the new level of total resources at the beginning of the period is given by

$$G_t = a_t + b_t + b_t^* + m_t \tag{2.52}$$

the Lagrangean function for the determination of the first-order conditions is modified to

$$V_t = \sum_{s=0}^{\infty} U(a_{t+s}, b_{t+s}, b_{t+s}^*, m_{t+s}) \frac{1}{(1+n)^s}$$

$$+ \psi (G_t - a_t - b_t - b_t^* - m_t) \tag{2.53}$$

Differentiation of (2.53) with respect to the endogenous variables yields the first-order conditions for an extremum:

$$\psi = U_a = U_b DF = U_{b^*} DF = U_m DF \tag{2.54}$$

The impact effect of a devaluation on the demand for *a*, *b*, *b** and *m* is described by

$$\frac{da}{de} = \frac{(b+m)\,|C_{51}|}{|J|} < 0 \tag{2.55}$$

$$\frac{db}{de} = \frac{(b+m)\,|C_{52}|}{|J|} < 0 \tag{2.56}$$

$$\frac{db^*}{de} = \frac{(b+m)\,|C_{53}|}{|J|} < 0 \tag{2.57}$$

$$\frac{dm}{de} = \frac{(b+m)\,|C_{54}|}{|J|} < 0 \tag{2.58}$$

The signs for the derivations reflect the fact that

$$|C_{51}|,\ |C_{52}|,\ |C_{53}|,\ |C_{54}| < 0 \qquad \text{and } |J| > 0$$

The effects on the respective excess demands are given by

$$\frac{dEDG}{de} = \frac{da}{de} - \frac{dy}{de} \equiv \frac{(b+m)\,|C_{51}|}{|J|} - 0 < 0 \tag{2.59}$$

$$\frac{dEDB}{de} = \frac{db^d}{de} - \frac{db^s}{de} \equiv \frac{(b+m)\,|C_{52}|}{|J|} + b > 0 \tag{2.60}$$

$$\frac{dEDB^*}{de} = \frac{db^{*d}}{de} - \frac{db^{*s}}{de} \equiv \frac{(b+m)\,|C_{53}|}{|J|} - 0 < 0 \tag{2.61}$$

$$\frac{dEDM}{de} = \frac{dm^d}{de} - \frac{dm^s}{de} \equiv \frac{(b+m)\,|C_{54}|}{|J|} + m > 0 \tag{2.62}$$

where the superscripts d and s refer to demand and supply, respectively.

Equations (2.59) through (2.62) indicate that the impact effect of a devaluation will be an excess supply of goods and foreign bonds and an excess demand for domestic bonds and money.

The size of the excess supplies/demands is determined by various factors. First, the larger the rate of time preference,[52] the smaller the excess supply of goods and foreign bonds as well as the excess demand for domestic bonds, and the larger the excess demand for money. Second, the larger the share of foreign bonds in a given size of total wealth, i.e., the smaller $(b + m)$, the smaller the reduction in spending (excess supply of goods) and the evolving excess supply of foreign bonds, and the larger the excess demand for domestic bonds and real balances. Finally, the larger the utility derived from real balances, i.e., the larger, ceteris paribus, the desired level of real balances and, thus, the smaller the initial income velocity of circulation, the larger the excess demand for money and the excess supplies of the other two assets.

Figure 2-8 describes in graphic form the adjustments in absorption and in the allocation of the wealth portfolio. Because of the small-country assumption, both the domestic price level (in terms of foreign currency) and the interest rate are invariably given. Hence, as opposed to the previous section both the absorption velocity, λ (and, therefore, the expansion path λ') and the income velocity, v, remain unaffected by the change in the exchange rate. Figure 2-8 demonstrates the consequences of a constant interest rate over time. Desired real wealth is given by $\bar{w}$ and remains unchanged throughout the entire process of adjustment. The constancy of the income velocity of circulation is expressed by the invariable line $0v$ through R. The rate at which individuals desire to return to equilibrium wealth is marked by the expansion path λ' through Q. Absorption velocity is given by the dashed λ line. Since domestic and foreign bonds are now internationally mobile and are considered by domestic and foreign residents to be perfect substitutes for each other, domestic and foreign bonds are subsumed in one unit. Their aggregate real value is expressed by the distance m_0w_0 on the ordinate.

A devaluation of the home country's currency has two distinct effects. On the one hand, it raises the price level by the percentage of the devaluation and,

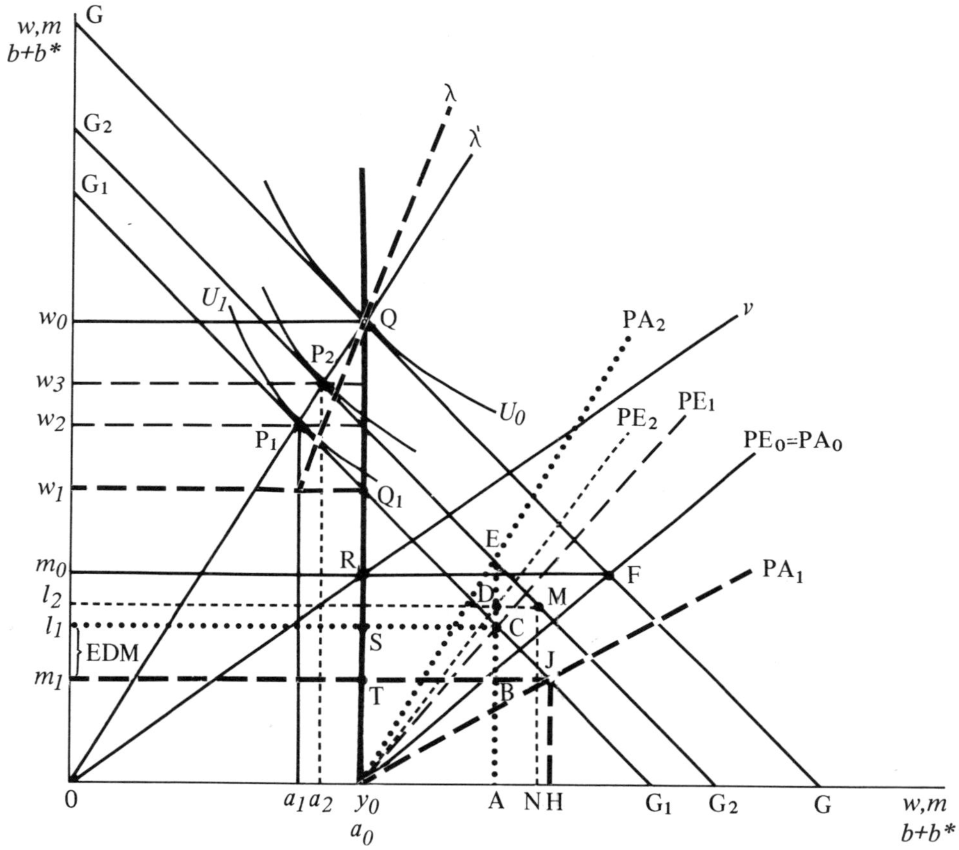

Figure 2-8. Spending and Portfolio Adjustments with Internationally Tradable Bonds.

thus, lowers real wealth. On the other hand, it raises the nominal value of foreign bonds held by domestic residents and, thus, increases their wealth. Provided goods arbitrage is perfect, the rise in the domestic price level will take place instantaneously, and, consequently, the net impact effect of the devaluation on real wealth is expressed by

$$\frac{dw}{de} = -(b + m) \equiv b^* - w \tag{2.63}$$

Hence, real wealth unambiguously declines except for the unlikely case in which domestic wealth consists entirely of foreign bonds. In this case a devaluation leaves real wealth unaffected. Consequently, the larger the share of foreign bonds in total wealth, the smaller the decline in real wealth for any given rate of depreciation of the domestic currency. After the devaluation real wealth is given by w_1. This new level of real wealth w_1 will lie closer to the original level w_0 the larger the share of foreign bonds in total wealth.

The decline in real wealth disturbs the initial balance between actual and desired real wealth and triggers adjustments in the spending behavior of economic agents. First-period equilibrium is obtained at point P_1. Absorption declines to a_1. In order to finance this level of absorption at an unchanged income velocity, economic agents require $0l_1$ = AC units of real balances. This implies a desired portfolio allocation expressed by the PE_1 line, with AG_1 = AC units of real balances and y_0A = Q_1S units of bonds. The actual allocation of the portfolio is, however, given by the PA_1 line with HG_1 = HJ units of real balances and y_0H = Q_1T units of bonds.

As a result of the divergence between the actual and the desired portfolio allocation, people will substitute real balances for bonds.[53] The exchange may take the form of sales of either domestic bonds or domestically owned foreign bonds to foreigners.[54] Whichever form is chosen, the result will be a surplus in the capital account equal to the excess demand for money $l_1 - m_1$ = BC = AH.[55]

As a result of the reduced level of domestic absorption, the home country will accrue a balance-of-trade surplus equal to the difference between the value of output and absorption; real wealth will rise by an equal amount.

In the left-hand panel of figure 2-8, the size of the trade-account surplus in real terms is equal to $y_0 - a_1$. Wealth rises by $w_2 - w_1$. In the right-hand panel, the balance-of-trade surplus and the change in real wealth is marked by CE = $w_2 - w_1$.

At the beginning of the next period, the country starts with real wealth equal to w_2 of which G_2A = AE (right-hand panel) consists of real balances. The actual allocation of assets in the portfolio is, therefore, expressed by the PA_2 ray through E.

Given the new level of wealth, the second-period utility maximum is given by the point of tangency P_2; the country desires to materialize a level of absorption equal to a_2. In order to finance this level of absorption, a level of real balances equal to $0l_2$ = AD = MN is required. In the second period, the country starts with an excess supply of real balances equal to ED. This excess supply is exchanged for bonds which are repurchased from foreigners. The capital account will, therefore, witness a surplus of an equal amount.

During the second period, the country will again run a balance-of-trade surplus which raises the level of real wealth. The trade-account surplus at the same time raises the level of actual real balances beyond the level required to finance the next period's desired absorption. The resulting excess supply of money will, therefore, be exchanged for bonds. This process will continue to work until actual real wealth once again reaches the level of desired wealth. During the process of adjustment, actual wealth and real bonds will return asymptotically to their equilibrium values. The rise in both magnitudes is effectuated by a domestic-saving process which produces trade-account surpluses. The size of the trade-account surplus will exceed that of the capital-account deficit. As actual wealth approaches the desired level, saving declines and the trade-account surpluses dwindle to zero. In equilibrium, real absorption will once again be equal to real income.

The individual subaccounts of the balance of payments develop in the following way: The adjustment in the first period involves a large capital-account surplus and a sizeable balance-of-trade surplus. In the second and all later periods, there will be a capital-account deficit and a trade-account surplus, both dwindling to zero as actual wealth approaches desired wealth. In the final equilibrium the home country will again experience a trade-account deficit and a service-account surplus of equal size;[56] the capital account and the balance of payments will be zero.

The development of the individual subbalances of the balance of payments is depicted in figure 2-9a, the development of real balances in figure 2-9b. In the example chosen, the service account goes into a deficit in the period after the devaluation because it is assumed that the replenishing of real balances after the devaluation up to the level required to finance the desired level of absorption requires the sale of all domestically owned foreign bonds plus the sale of domestic debt instruments to foreigners. The dotted line in figure 2-9b, below the solid line representing the development of the money supply, points to the fact that the money supply is regularly adjusted to the levels of real balances desired in each period (denoted by l_1, l_2, . . .) via purchases of bonds.

It is obvious that given the level of real wealth in each period the level of real balances required to finance desired absorption in each period will determine the share of interest-earning assets in the portfolio. This follows unambiguously from the wealth constraint. As such, there exists an interdependence between the decision about the level of spending and the allocation of the portfolio. As savers, people decide how much to add to their wealth in order to regain the desired wealth position. This decision determines absorption velocity and is based on the internal rate of time preference as well as on the interest rate. As portfolio managers, people decide how to distribute their wealth among various assets, including their real balances. Given real income and absorption, this decision is based entirely on the rate of nonpecuniary and/or productive services of money and the rates of return on capital and other assets. As absorption (income) varies due to, e.g., a change in the exchange rate, the financing requirements change, and the desired proportion of real balances in total wealth will be adjusted accordingly. For this reason it does not seem to be appropriate to assume that spending and portfolio decisions are entirely independent of each other.[57]

While in the previous section, which did not allow for the trade of either domestic or foreign bonds, the adjustment toward equilibrium involved interest-rate changes and ensuing adjustments in the demand for goods and money, this

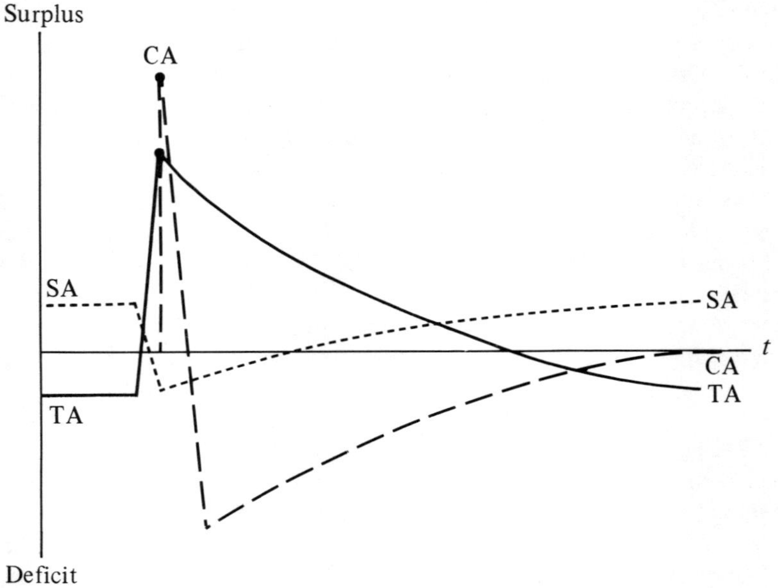

Figure 2-9a. Adjustments in the Trade, Capital, and Service Accounts after Devaluation. (TA = Trade account; CA = Capital Account; SA = Service Account).

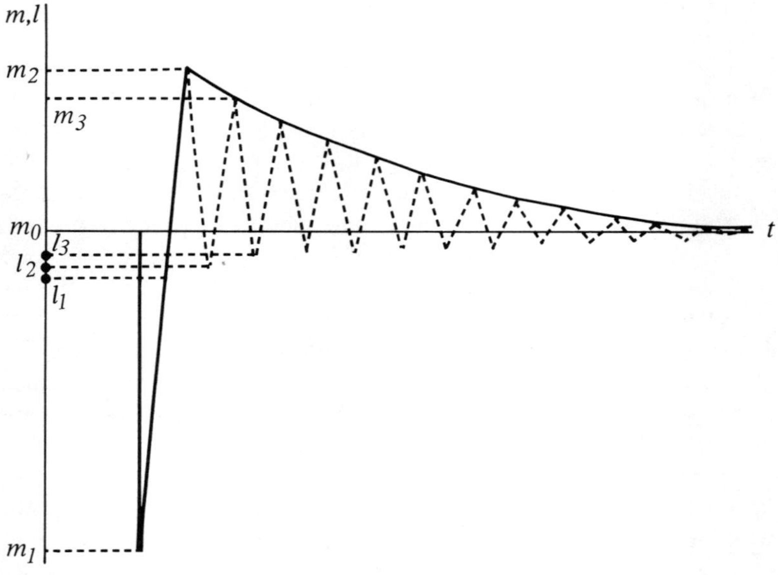

Figure 2-9b. Adjustment of Real Balances after a Devaluation (Capital Movements Permitted).

section highlights the smoothing effect of capital flows on adjustments in the goods and money markets. In reality both effects, the interest effect and the capital-flow effect, must be assumed to operate simultaneously. Their relative strength will depend upon the share of nontraded bonds in total interest-bearing assets of an economy and the degree of substitutability between tradable assets as well as the degree of capital mobility. The latter aspects are often heavily influenced by the degree and nature of capital controls and other barriers to a free trade of financial assets.

Furthermore, it has been demonstrated in this section that the incorporation of domestic and foreign bonds as internationally tradable assets does not impinge on the main result obtained in the previous analyses, which concentrated on goods and money as the only tradable items: a devaluation results only in a temporary, not in a permanent, improvement of the balance of payments. During the process of adjustment both the current and the capital account contribute to balance-of-payments surpluses. The costs of adjustment in the form of information and transactions costs are usually lower in asset markets than in goods markets. As a result the former generally displays a higher degree of flexibility and must therefore be expected to bear the brunt of the adjustment in the first period(s) after a devaluation. The capital account will fully reflect this phenomenon.

A devaluation does not change the balance of payments in the long run but does cause a permanent increase in the stock of foreign reserves and thus, barring active and permanent neutralizing actions of the domestic central bank, a permanent increase in the money supply. In equilibrium, the percentage change in reserves and in the supply of money will be equal to the percentage change in the price level, which, in turn, will be equal to the rate of devaluation of the domestic currency.

A permanent imbalance in the balance of payments after a devaluation is possible only if one or more determinants of the actual and/or desired level of wealth and money is continuously changed in response to, or along with, the devaluation.

One such possibility is a continuous adjustment in net domestic assets by the central bank in an attempt to offset the expansionary effects of the rise in foreign reserves. In a stationary economy, the intervention of the central bank cannot, however, last forever because in a country running a surplus in its balance of payments, the central bank will soon have depleted its stock of marketable domestic credit papers. In a deficit country, the central bank will eventually exhaust its stock of international reserves. But even in growing economies there will be only limited scope for successful intervention by the central bank in the long run.

Another theoretical possibility for a permanent change in the balance of payments is a continuous adjustment in the demand for money/wealth induced by the devaluation. It has been demonstrated above that the long-run levels of the determinants of the demand for money or wealth remain unaffected by a change in the exchange rate. A recurrent adjustment in the demand functions is thereby excluded, and, consequently, a change in the exchange rate will have only temporary effects on the balance of payments.

3 Devaluation and Portfolio Adjustment

Presentation of the Model

The preceding chapter incorporated capital movements into the analysis of a devaluation. It remained restrictive, however, in that it maintained the small-country assumption. Furthermore, it was assumed that the two forms of interest-earning assets were perfect substitutes for one another and that perfect capital mobility existed. Taken together, these assumptions implied that there was no leeway for the domestic interest rate to vary over time and to deviate from the foreign rate.

The fixity of the domestic interest rate after a devaluation does not correspond to observations in the real world. In addition, it bars the analysis of a number of important adjustment processes on the part of the public. To the extent that economic policy measures respond to variations in the behavior of the public and to the corresponding variations in certain economic variables, it also bars the analysis of the effects of these policy measures and their influence on the success of a devaluation.

Central variables that are affected by adjustments in the domestic interest rate are the level of desired wealth, absorption velocity, and the income velocity of circulation. The analysis of changes in the domestic interest rate will be carried out in a portfolio equilibrium model which incorporates the repercussions of portfolio adjustments and interest rate variations on the equilibrium in commodity markets.

A variation in the domestic interest rate is made analytically possible by relaxing either of the two above assumptions: the small-country assumption or the assumption of perfect substitutability between domestic and foreign interest-earning assets. Relaxation of the small-country assumption implies that any incipient domestic excess demand for either domestic or foreign bonds will change its price and, thus, the domestic and world interest rate. Relaxation of the assumption of perfect substitutability implies that a difference between the domestic and the foreign interest rate is possible—even in the long run—because of, e.g., differential risk attributed to the two assets.

In the subsequent analysis, the latter approach is chosen because dropping the small-country assumption would also affect the determination of the domestic price level, which has so far been conveniently treated as being exogenously determined by the price level of the rest of the world. Thus, dropping the small-country assumption would largely complicate the diagrammatic presentation as well as the algebra without adding to the analysis of portfolio behavior and its interaction with spending decisions.

Assume that domestic asset holders have demand functions for three imperfectly substitutable assets:[1] money (M), domestic bonds (B), and foreign bonds (B^*). Since domestic bonds are assumed to be a nontradable asset, residents must hold a given stock of B. On the other hand, they are free to trade between money and foreign bonds. The markets for money and foreign bonds are assumed to be so large that any incipient demand for M and B^* does not affect their price[2] (small-country assumption). The infinitely elastic supply of B^*, for example, ensures that any domestic demand for foreign bonds is met at a fixed interest rate r^*.

Nominal wealth (W) of domestic residents is equal to the sum of the three above assets

$$W = M + B + eB^* \tag{3.1}$$

where eB^* is the domestic currency value of foreign bonds owned by domestic residents.

The demand for each asset is a function of the respective rates of return r and r^*, and income Y. Income is included to represent the transactions demand for money.[3]

Equilibrium in the three asset markets obtains when

$$M = F^M (r, r^*, Y)\, W \tag{3.2}$$

$$B = F^B (r, r^*, Y)\, W \tag{3.3}$$

$$eB^* = F^{B^*} (r, r^*, Y)\, W \tag{3.4}$$

F^M, F^B and F^{B^*} represent the desired shares of the respective asset in total nominal wealth W given r, r^* and Y. By the wealth constraint the shares must add up to one

$$F^M + F^B + F^{B^*} = 1$$

A corollary to this is the fact that the partial derivatives of the distribution functions F^i with respect to each argument j must add up to zero, e.g.,

$$F^M_r + F^B_r + F^{B^*}_r = 0$$

or, alternatively,

$$F_r^B = -F_r^M - F_r^{B*}$$

Though imperfectly substitutable, the three assets are considered gross substitutes. This implies that the partial derivative of a demand function with respect to its own argument is positive; it is negative with respect to an alien argument, e.g.,

$$F_Y^M > 0, \qquad F_r^M, F_{r*}^M < 0$$

The equilibrium curves for each asset market are derived by first differentiating equations (3.2) to (3.4) and then rearranging items while observing the wealth constraint (3.1). The equilibrium curves are given by

$$\text{MM:} \quad WF_r^M dr = -WF_{r*}^M dr* - WF_Y^M dY + (1 - F^M)\, dm$$
$$-F^M dB - F^M d\,(eB*)$$

$$\text{BB:} \quad WF_r^B dr = -WF_{r*}^B dr* - WF_Y^B dY + (1 - F^B)\, dB$$
$$-F^B dM - F^B d\,(eB*)$$

$$\text{B*B*:} \quad WF_r^{B*} dr = -WF_{r*}^{B*} dr* - WF_Y^B dY + (1 - F^{B*})\, d(eB*)$$
$$-F^{B*} dM - F^{B*} dB$$

In a diagram which measures the domestic interest rate and domestic nominal income as dependent variables on its axes[4], the slopes of the curves expressing equilibrium in the respective markets are determined by

$$\left.\frac{dr}{dY}\right|_{MM} = -\frac{F_Y^M}{F_r^M} > 0$$

$$\left.\frac{dr}{dY}\right|_{BB} = -\frac{F_Y^B}{F_r^B} > 0$$

$$\left.\frac{dr}{dY}\right|_{B*B*} = -\frac{F_Y^{B*}}{F_r^{B*}} < 0$$

The MM schedule is positively sloped, since a rise in domestic income raises the demand for nominal balances and the domestic interest rate must rise in order to reestablish equilibrium. The BB schedule is also positively sloped since a rise in income raises transactions demand for money and, thus, lowers the demand for bonds; a rise in the interest rate is required for equilibrium in the domestic bond market. The B*B* schedule is negatively sloped, since a rise in income raises transactions demand for money and lowers the demand for foreign bonds; the domestic interest rate must fall in order to raise demand for foreign bonds and thereby restore equilibrium in the foreign bond market.

Since $F_Y^M > F_Y^B$ and $F_r^M < F_r^B$, the slope of the MM curve must be steeper than the slope of the BB curve.[5] This reflects the fact that demand for money is more responsive to changes in income than the demand for bonds, whereas the latter is more responsive to changes in the interest rate than the former.

The equilibrium schedules for the three markets are depicted in figure 3-1. The relation between the three markets is best understood when it is recognized that in a system of fixed exchange rates, any purchase of foreign bonds will necessarily reduce and any sale will increase domestic reserves by that amount. By assuming a stable money multiplier, the money supply changes by a multiple of the change in reserves. Any direct substitution between M and B^* will leave the desired quantity of B unaffected. Consequently, the analysis can be reduced to a two-part wealth, or balance sheet, constraint:[6]

$$W = H + B \tag{3.5}$$

where

$$H = M + eB^* \tag{3.6}$$

Substitution of equations (3.2) and (3.4) into (3.6) yields

$$H = F^M (r, r^*, Y) W + F^{B^*} (r, r^*, Y) W \tag{3.7}$$

There are now two portfolio balance equations left, (3.3) and (3.7), which are constrained by equation (3.5) so that only one of them is an independent equation determining the domestic interest rate r, given B, e, B^*, M, r^* and Y. Any one of the two equations will suffice to determine portfolio equilibrium in the system. Since the behavior of the domestic interest rate is of particular interest here, the subsequent analysis will focus on the equilibrium in the domestic bond market. The special importance of the domestic bond market is emphasized by the fact that the BB curve is drawn as a heavy solid line in figure 3-1. For an analysis of the behavior of the domestic interest rate in response to a devaluation it would suffice to observe the domestic bond market. However, both the equilibrium line for the money market and the foreign bond-market line will generally appear in the figures in this chapter in order to demonstrate what adjustments take place in the money market as well as in the market for foreign

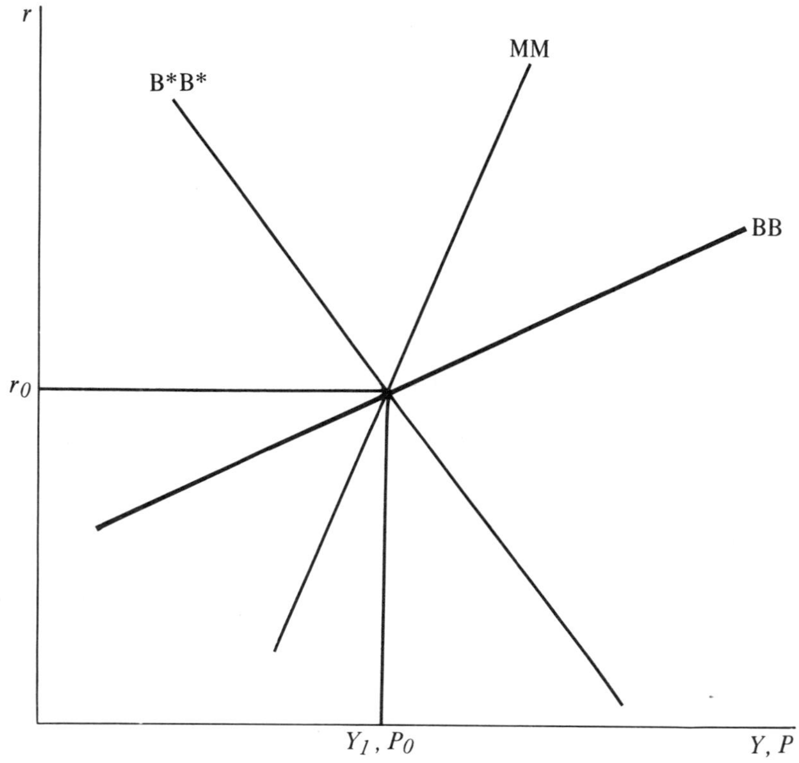

Figure 3-1. Portfolio Equilibrium with Money and Domestic and Foreign Bonds.

bonds. Trade in the latter market is important because it entails capital movements and, thus, affects the balance of payments.

Since foreign bonds are in elastic supply at a fixed interest rate r^*, the system of portfolio balance equations is recursive. Hence, either equation (3.3) or (3.7) can be solved for the domestic interest rate. The equation obtained for the interest rate can then be substituted into equations (3.2) and (3.4) to obtain the solutions for equilibrium money demand and equilibrium demand for foreign bonds with no feedback onto the domestic interest rate.

In order to investigate the determinants of the domestic interest rate, differentiate totally equation (3.3) to obtain

$$dr = -\frac{F^B_{r^*}}{F^B_r}\,dr^* - \frac{F^B_Y}{F^B_r}\,dY + \frac{(1 - F^B)}{WF^B_r}\,dB - \frac{F^B}{WF^B_r}\,dM - \frac{F^B}{WF^B_r}\,d\,(eB^*) \qquad (3.8)$$

Notice that by virtue of the wealth constraint

$$F^B_r = -F^M_r - F^{B*}_r ; F^B_{r*} = - F^M_{r*} - F^{B*}_{r*} ; F^B_Y = - F^M_Y - F^{B*}_Y$$

Furthermore,

$$F^B = 1 - F^M - F^{B*}$$

In analyzing the effects of changes in exogenous variables on *r*, any of these substitutions may hence be made if this helps the understanding of the effects of changes in the right-hand variables of (3.8) on *r*.

Next differentiate totally equations (3.2) and (3.4) and substitute equation (3.8) for *dr* to obtain the determinants of the demand for money and the demand for foreign bonds. Changes in the demand for money depend on

$$\begin{aligned} dM = {} & W\left(F^M_{r*} - F^M_r \frac{F^B_{r*}}{F^B_r}\right) dr* \\ & + W\left(F^M_Y - F^M_r \frac{F^B_{Y*}}{F^B_r}\right) dY \\ & + \left[F^M + (1 - F^B)\frac{F^M_r}{F^B_r}\right] dB + \left(F^M - F^B \frac{F^M_r}{F^B_r}\right) dH \end{aligned} \tag{3.9}$$

while variations in the desired value of foreign bonds are determined by

$$\begin{aligned} d\,(eB*)^d = {} & W\left(F^{B*}_{r*} - F^B_{r*} \frac{F^{B*}_r}{F^B_r}\right) dr* \\ & + W\left(F^{B*}_Y - F^B_Y \frac{F^{B*}_r}{F^B_r}\right) dY \\ & + \left[F^{B*} + (1 - F^B)\frac{F^{B*}_r}{F^B_r}\right] dB \\ & + \left(F^{B*} - F^B \frac{F^{B*}_r}{F^B_r}\right) dH \end{aligned} \tag{3.10}$$

where $dH = dM + d(eB*)$.

Effects of a Change in the Exchange Rate

Money as a Producer's Good

It is now possible to analyze the impact effects of a change in the exchange rate on the domestic interest rate, the demand for money, and the demand for foreign bonds.

The first-period change in the domestic interest rate after a devaluation is expressed by[7]

$$\frac{dr}{de} = -\frac{F_Y^B}{F_r^B} y - \frac{F^B}{WF_r^B} B^* \tag{3.11}$$

The first-period change in the demand for money is denoted by

$$\frac{dM}{de} = W\left(F_Y^M - F_r^M \frac{F_Y^B}{F_r^B}\right) y + \left(F^M - F^B \frac{F_r^M}{F_r^B}\right) B^* \tag{3.12}$$

Demand for foreign bonds changes by

$$\frac{d(eB^*)^d}{de} = W\left(F_Y^{B^*} - F_Y^B \frac{F_r^{B^*}}{F_r^B}\right) y + \left(F^{B^*} - F^B \frac{F_r^{B^*}}{F_r^B}\right) B^* \tag{3.13}$$

while at the same time the money value of the stock of foreign bonds (eB^*) increases by

$$\frac{d(eB^*)}{de} = B^* \tag{3.14}$$

The value of nominal wealth is thereby increased by an equal amount. Each of the changes in the variables r, M and $(eB^*)^d$ can be broken down into two separate influences. The first is the change in the respective variable due to the change in nominal wealth. This influence is always measured by the terms or the sum in brackets multiplied by B^*. It represents the nominal wealth effect on the variable under consideration. The second is the influence of the exchange rate on the domestic price level and thus, on the nominal value of output that must be financed.[8] This second influence represents, consequently, the effects of a higher transactions demand for money on portfolio equilibrium; it is always denoted by the sum in brackets multiplied by y.

Whereas the first influence captures the effects on asset demand of a change in a scale variable, the latter influence represents the effects of a change in a factor affecting the allocation of a given portfolio of assets. It may be useful to consider these two influences separately in order to evaluate which disequilibrium situations they create and which adjustment processes follow from them. Consider first the impact effects of the change in nominal wealth on portfolio equilibrium.

A devaluation raises the value of domestically owned foreign bonds by the same percentage:

$$\frac{d(eB^*)}{eB^*} = de/e$$

As a result, nominal wealth increases by a percentage which depends on the share of foreign bonds in domestic wealth:[9]

$$dW/W = F^{B^*}\, de/e$$

Figure 3-2 describes the first-period stock adjustment process. The initial stock-and-flow equilibrium is represented by point R. At R all three asset markets are in equilibrium; hence, stock equilibrium obtains. The equilibrium level of nominal wealth is $W_0 = M_0 + B_0 + e_0B_0^*$. For expository purposes R is taken as a reference point for the relative changes in nominal wealth which take place during the adjustment process. R also represents flow equilibrium since, by assumption, nominal demand ($A_0 = a_0P_0$) is equal to nominal supply at the initial price level P_0 and exchange rate e_0. As in the case of nominal wealth, R serves as a reference point for the relative changes in P and e. Consequently, in addition to nominal income, the domestic price level, the exchange rate, and nominal wealth can be measured on the abscissa.[10] The devaluation-induced increase in the value of foreign bonds is represented by the shift of what may be dubbed the "foreign bond supply curve" $B^*B^*_{1S}$ to point T. The corresponding increase in nominal wealth is indicated by the movement of the point measuring wealth from W_0 to W_1 (R to S). The larger the share of foreign bonds in domestic wealth, the closer S will be to T. Real wealth would be restored at its old level, if the price level increased by the same percentage as nominal wealth. If the home country is a net debtor, points T and S will be located to the left of R, indicating the decline in both nominal and real wealth as a result of the devaluation. In this case the domestic price level will have to decline in order to restore the old level of real wealth. In the case of a country which is a net lender, the impact effect of an increase in the scale variable nominal wealth induces an increase in the demand for all three assets [compare equations (3.2) to (3.4)]. This change in the demand for the three assets is depicted by a rightward shift of the curves that

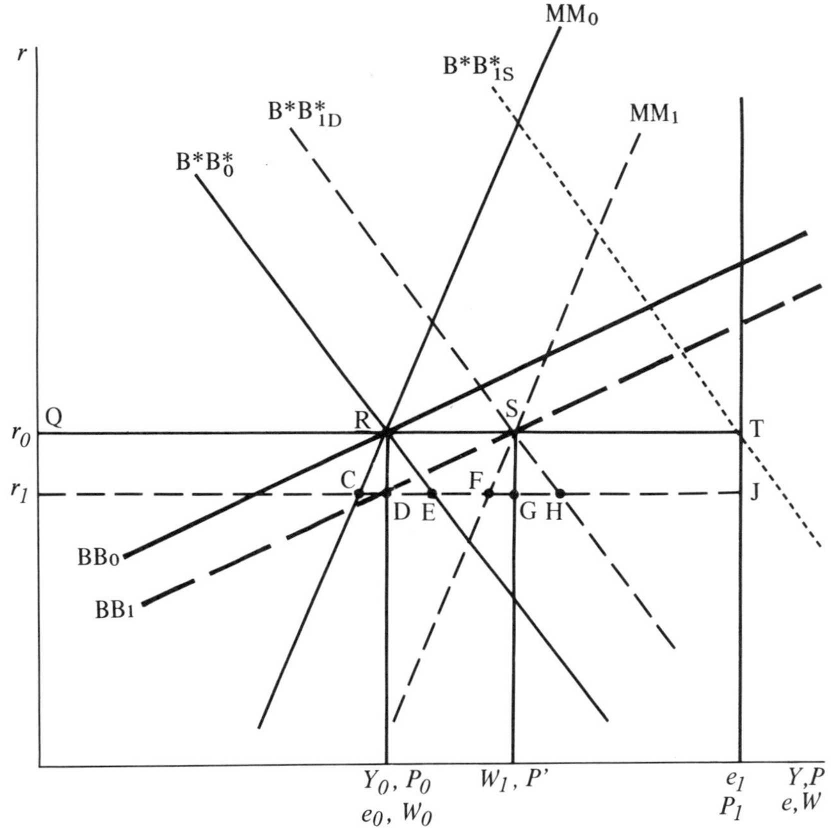

Figure 3-2. Devaluation and Portfolio Disequilibria.

represent the equilibrium in the markets for the three assets. The size of the increase in the demand for the individual assets is given by the distances between MM_0 and MM_1 for the money market, BB_0 - BB_1 for the domestic bond market, and $B^*B_0^*$ - $B^*B_{1D}^*$ for the foreign bond market, respectively.[11]

Equations (3.12) and (3.13) point to the various factors which determine the size of the instantaneous excess demand for money and the change in the demand for foreign bonds. For example, in equation (3.13), the term in brackets, which is multiplied by B^*, indicates that the excess demand for money will be larger, the larger the elasticity of demand for money with respect to the domestic interest rate. From equation (3.13) it follows that the change in the demand for foreign bonds will be larger, the larger the degree of substitutability between domestic and foreign bonds.

In order to establish the size of the excess demand for foreign bonds, the change in the demand for these bonds as given by equation (3.13) has to be netted against the devaluation-induced change in its "supply," i.e., in the value of the existing stock of foreign bonds [compare equation (3.14)]. Looking at the wealth effect only, the excess demand is given by

$$EDB^* = B^* \left(F^{B^*} - F^B \frac{F_r^{B^*}}{F_r^B} - 1 \right)$$

Because the term in brackets is smaller than zero, it is demonstrated that the wealth effect of a devaluation creates an excess supply of foreign bonds if the country is a net international lender, i.e., if B^* is positive. In figure 3-2, the size of this excess supply of foreign bonds is indicated by the distance between $B^*B^*_{1D}$ and $B^*B^*_{1S}$, e.g., ST for the initial interest rate.

Before any change in the domestic price level and the rate of interest has taken place, the wealth effect of a devaluation will thus lead to an excess demand for money and domestic bonds and will cause an excess supply of foreign bonds, provided the home country is a net owner of foreign capital. The wealth effect on the demand for domestic bonds meets with an inelastic supply. Thus any incipient excess demand for domestic bonds will raise their price and lower the rate of interest. The nominal value of the stock of domestic bonds increases by the same percentage as its price. The decline of the domestic interest rate which follows solely from the portfolio adjustment in response to the rise in nominal wealth—neglecting the price effect—is denoted by equation (3.11) where

$$dr = -\frac{F^B B^*}{WF_r^B} de < 0$$

or, since $F^{B^*} = eB^*/W$, and assuming that $e = 1$ initially,

$$dr = -\frac{F^B F^{B^*}}{F_r^B} de < 0$$

Given the share of domestic bonds in wealth F^B, the domestic interest rate is seen to decline more, the smaller the interest elasticity of domestic bonds and the larger the share of foreign bonds in wealth, F^{B^*}, i.e., the larger the increase in nominal wealth.

The impact effect of the rise in nominal wealth, and the corresponding excess demand for domestic bonds on the domestic interest rate is indicated in figure 3-2 by the decline of r from r_0 to r_1. Recall again that this result holds for a net creditor country. In a net debtor country, the wealth effect will generate an increase in the domestic interest rate.

The decline in the domestic interest rate restores the equilibrium in the domestic bond market at point D but generates further disturbances in the markets for money and foreign bonds.[12] The demand for money rises by FG (= CD), while the demand for foreign bonds rises by GH. The overall excess demand for money hence rises from its wealth-induced magnitude RS (= DG) to the wealth-cum-interest-effect level CG while the initial excess supply of foreign bonds is reduced from ST (= GJ) to the wealth-cum-interest-effect magnitude of HJ.

With reference to figure 2-6 the change in the demand for money can be explained as follows: The rise in wealth to, say, w_Z raises equilibrium absorption to a_Z and—at an unchanged velocity—the demand for money to l_Z. As the domestic interest rate declines in response to wealth-induced purchases of domestic bonds, the velocity of circulation declines to v_2, and the demand for money increases further to its wealth-cum-interest-effect level l'_Z.

In an attempt to achieve portfolio equilibrium, domestic residents will trade in foreign bonds for money. As a result of this transaction the home country will experience a capital-account surplus, the net foreign asset component of the monetary base, and thus the money supply will rise. The adjustment in the domestic money supply will enable domestic residents to finance the desired increase in absorption. The rise in expenditure, in turn, will result in a general price rise since the increase in the demand for goods and services meets with an inelastic supply.[13]

As the price level and nominal income rise, and the demand for domestic and foreign bonds declines and the demand for money rises. The decline in the demand for domestic bonds generates a rise in their return; the decline in the demand for foreign bonds results in further capital inflows. Assuming that throughout the process of adjustment portfolio equilibrium obtains in the domestic bond market, the economy will move from point D along the BB_1 line toward point S. The adjustment involves a continuous rise in both the domestic interest rate and the price level. Equilibrium obtains at point S where the price level has risen by the same percentage as nominal wealth; all real magnitudes will be restored to their predevaluation level.

Assume now that the portfolio adjustment in response to the (nominal) wealth effect[14] of a devaluation is completed and consider the effect of a devaluation on the domestic price level. Given perfect arbitrage, the domestic price level will rise instantaneously by the percentage of the devaluation and so will nominal income (= the value of domestic output). In figure 3-3 this is indicated by the shift of Y from Y_0 to Y_1. The increase in nominal income, in turn, raises the transactions demand for money such that the effective demand for money after the change in the value of output is expressed by the MM_2 schedule running through T. Equation (3.12) indicates that the size of the excess demand for money (ST) (previous to an adjustment in the domestic interest rate and excluding the wealth effect)

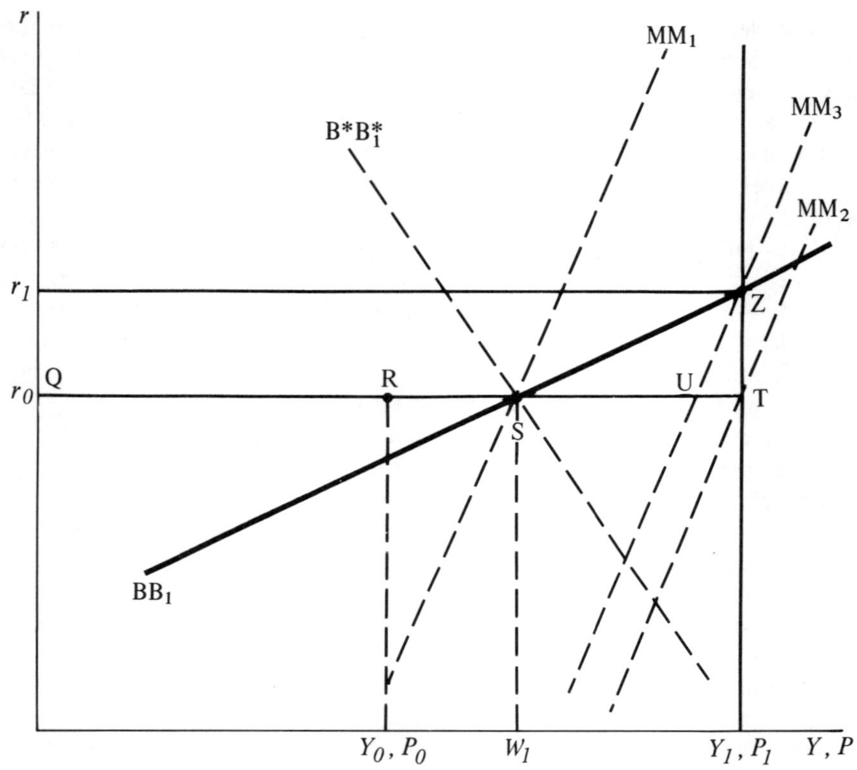

Figure 3-3. Interest Rate Adjustment after a Devaluation (Money Treated as a Producer's Good).

$$dM = W\, F_Y^M\, y\, de$$

depends primarily on the responsiveness of money demand with respect to changes in income F_Y^M. The excess demand will be larger, the larger F_Y^M. In terms of figure 3-3, this means that the excess demand will be larger, the steeper the slope of MM. Recall that for demonstration purposes the scale (wealth) effect on portfolio allocation has been dissociated from the effect of a change in a distribution factor (current nominal income) of the demand functions for the three assets. ST is thus the excess demand for money after the adjustment to the change in wealth has already taken place. The overall excess demand for money resulting from a devaluation is given by RT.

By virtue of the portfolio-balance equations (3.2) to (3.4), the excess demand for money implies an excess supply of both domestic and foreign bonds.

The excess supply of foreign bonds follows from equation (3.13) and is denoted by

$$d(eB^*)^d = WF_Y^{B^*} y\, de$$

for the case of a constant domestic interest rate. As a result of the small-country assumption, money balances can be exchanged for foreign bonds at a constant price, i.e., the sale of foreign bonds by domestic residents will not affect the foreign interest rate.

This is not true for domestic bonds. The aggregate attempt to sell off domestic bonds will cause their price to decline and their yield to increase to a point where domestic residents are willing to hold the existing stock of bonds. Starting from point *S*, the point at which the wealth-determined portfolio adjustment is completed, the interest rate will rise to r_1. The magnitude of the increase in the domestic interest rate due to the increase in the transactions demand for money is indicated by the first part of equation (3.11)

$$dr = -\frac{F_Y^B}{F_r^B} y\, de$$

The right-hand term is unambiguously positive: the interest rate rises due to this influence. It is observed that the rise in the domestic interest rate is larger the greater the degree of substitutability between money and domestic bonds. If F_Y^B is zero no change in the domestic interest rate will take place.[15] Capital inflows will be smaller in this case than in the case of a rising domestic interest rate.[16]

If, on the other hand, domestic bonds are almost entirely illiquid in the short run, F_Y^B effectively approaches infinity; the domestic interest rate will have to rise sharply in order to overcome the illiquidity. As a result capital inflows will loom large.

This result follows immediately from the fact that a rising domestic interest rate generates a second kind of substitution over and above the initial substitution of money for foreign bonds; namely, a substitution between domestic and foreign bonds. Capital inflows from this source will be higher, the higher the substitutability between domestic and foreign bonds, i.e., the higher the ratio $F_r^{B^*}/F_r^B$.

Another effect which follows the rise in the domestic interest rate relates to the demand for money. As the interest rate rises, the opportunity costs of holding money balances increase. As a result, people will feel inclined to reduce their demand for money. The effect of the rise in the domestic interest rate on transactions demand for money is denoted by the term $F_r^M\ F_{r*}^B/F_r^B$ in equation (3.12). This term is positive. Given the minus sign in front of it, it is clear that the overall transactions demand for money will decline as a result of the rise in the domestic interest rate. In figure 3-3, the reduction in the demand for money is indicated by the leftward shift in the MM schedule from MM_2 to MM_3.

It is obvious that a lower level of money balances as indicated by MM_3 is able to finance the given value of output Y_1 only if velocity rises. The shift from MM_2 to MM_3 may, thus, be correctly interpreted as a rise in the income velocity of circulation of money.

The results of the above analysis may be summarized as follows: A change in the exchange rate will bring about two distinct forms of adjustment in the portfolio of assets held by residents of a country. The first reflects the effects of a change in the scale of the portfolio; the second is-the result of a change in an argument in the demand functions for the various assets.

A devaluation is seen to raise the domestic currency value of all assets denominated in foreign currency. The effect of this change is twofold: it disturbs the balance between asset holdings in the portfolio and it raises the level of nominal wealth. Given constancy in the arguments of the asset-demand functions, the ensuing adjustment process will reestablish the old ratios between assets.

The second type of adjustment in the portfolio is the result of the fact that a devaluation raises nominal income via an increase in the price level. As a result transactions demand for money rises. The ensuing stock adjustment process establishes the new desired asset ratios. The transactions-demand effect works against the wealth effect in the case of demand for domestic and foreign bonds; in the case of the demand for money it works in a complementary fashion.

The two types of adjustment processes entail capital inflows which will be larger, the larger the rise in the domestic interest rate. The rise in the latter, in turn, depends crucially on the degree of liquidity of domestic bonds which determines the de facto substitutability between money and domestic bonds.

An additional result of the rise in the domestic interest rate is an increase in the velocity of circulation of money which will lower the amount of money required to finance a given level of nominal income.

Instantaneous equilibrium of the first period is denoted by point Z in figure 3-3. All three asset markets are in equilibrium (B*B* curve not drawn) and the level of output can be financed by the given stock of money.

Money as a Consumer's Good

The treatment of money as a producer's good bars the analysis from a number of interesting insights into decision-making processes on the part of the public. In particular, the interdependence between asset-market equilibria and spending decisions is blurred. As was established before, absorption velocity, and thus the level of spending in each period during the adjustment process, is influenced by the rate of interest. Therefore, if the adjustment toward asset-market equilibrium involves a change in the domestic interest rate, one should expect the public to revise its spending decisions. This revision in spending, in turn, changes the transactions demand for money with ensuing effects on portfolio equilibrium and the rate of interest. In addition, any variation in the interest rate influences the level of wealth desired by the public. Hence, one should expect an additional adjustment to follow from this source of imbalance in the system.

In order to study the kind and the magnitude of the above influences, money is now treated as a medium of exchange in the goods markets rather than as a factor of production, and the demand for nominal money balances is consequently assumed to depend on nominal absorption A rather than on nominal income Y. The asset-demand functions (3.2) to (3.4) are changed so that they include A as an argument instead of Y. In all other equations relating to portfolio adjustment processes the corresponding adjustments are made.

Central to the following analysis of the path of adjustment in major variables is the behavior of the domestic interest rate over time. Because of the two-part wealth constraint, either equation (3.3) or equation (3.7) can be solved for the domestic interest rate. The effect of a change in the exchange rate on the domestic interest rate is denoted by the general solution

$$WF_r^B \frac{dr}{de} = -WF_A^B \frac{dA}{de} - F^B \frac{d(eB^*)}{de} \tag{3.15}$$

Since $A = a \times P$, it follows that

$$\frac{dA}{de} = P\frac{da}{de} + a\frac{dP}{de} \tag{3.16}$$

Given perfect arbitrage dP/de equals unity. The derivation of real absorption with respect to the exchange rate is obtained by recalling that

$$a = y + \lambda\ (r,n)\ [w - \bar{w}\ (r,r^*)] \tag{3.17}$$

Equation (3.17) is a modification of equation (2.50); it includes the results of previous reasoning, namely that both absorption velocity and the desired level of wealth are influenced by the domestic interest rate. The marginal rate of time preference n and the foreign interest rate r^* are still considered exogenously given so that they do not respond to a change in the exchange rate. On the other hand, the domestic interest rate is allowed to vary with a change in the exchange rate. As has been demonstrated in the previous section, variations in the interest rate follow from adjustments in the portfolio of assets of domestic residents.

Differentiation of equation (3.17) with respect to the exchange rate yields[17]

$$\frac{da}{de} = \frac{\delta\lambda}{\delta r}\frac{dr}{de}\left[(b^* - w) - \frac{\delta w}{\delta r}\right] + \lambda(b^* - w) - \lambda\frac{\delta\bar{w}}{\delta r}\frac{dr}{de} \tag{3.18}$$

The first-period change in nominal absorption after a devaluation is given by

$$\frac{dA}{de} = \left\{\frac{\delta\lambda}{\delta r}\left[(b^* - w) - \frac{\delta w}{\delta r}\right] - \lambda\frac{\delta w}{\delta r}\right\}\frac{dr}{de} + \lambda(b^* - w) + a \tag{3.19}$$

Equilibrium in the goods markets is represented by the AA lines in figure 3-4. Initially nominal absorption A_0 is equal to nominal income Y_0. This is demonstrated by the fact that the line depicting the initial equilibrium in the goods markets, AA_0, intersects the "interest line" at R. The AA lines are seen to depend negatively on the rate of interest. As the rate of interest rises, absorption declines;[18] it requires a decline in the price level in order to restore real absorption to its former level.

The impact effect of the devaluation, i.e., before any change in the domestic interest rate has taken place, raises nominal absorption to A_1. The size of this effect is given by the two last terms in equation (3.19). It is observed that nominal absorption rises by less than the value of output as long as b^* is smaller than w

$$\frac{dA}{de} = \lambda(b^* - w) + a < \frac{dY}{de} = y \equiv a$$

Furthermore, the rise in nominal absorption will be stronger, and hence the rightward shift of the AA curve larger, the larger the share of foreign bonds in total wealth, i.e., the smaller $(b^* - w)$. This implies that the first-period trade surplus will be inversely related to the share of foreign bonds in wealth. Equation (3.19) suggests, in addition, that the trade surplus will be positively related to absorption velocity λ.

In figure 3-4 the change in nominal income is given by RT and the incipient change in nominal absorption (i.e., before any adjustment in the interest rate) is indicated by RS.

Equation (3.19) suggests that any rise in the interest rate above r_0 will lower nominal absorption below A_1 for two reasons. First, the rise in the interest rate will distrub the initial balance between the marginal rate of time preference and the interest rate. It will consequently affect the intertemporal distribution of expenditure and thus raise absorption velocity and thereby lower absorption of any given period during the adjustment process. This effect is represented by the first term of equation (3.19). It is negative as r rises.

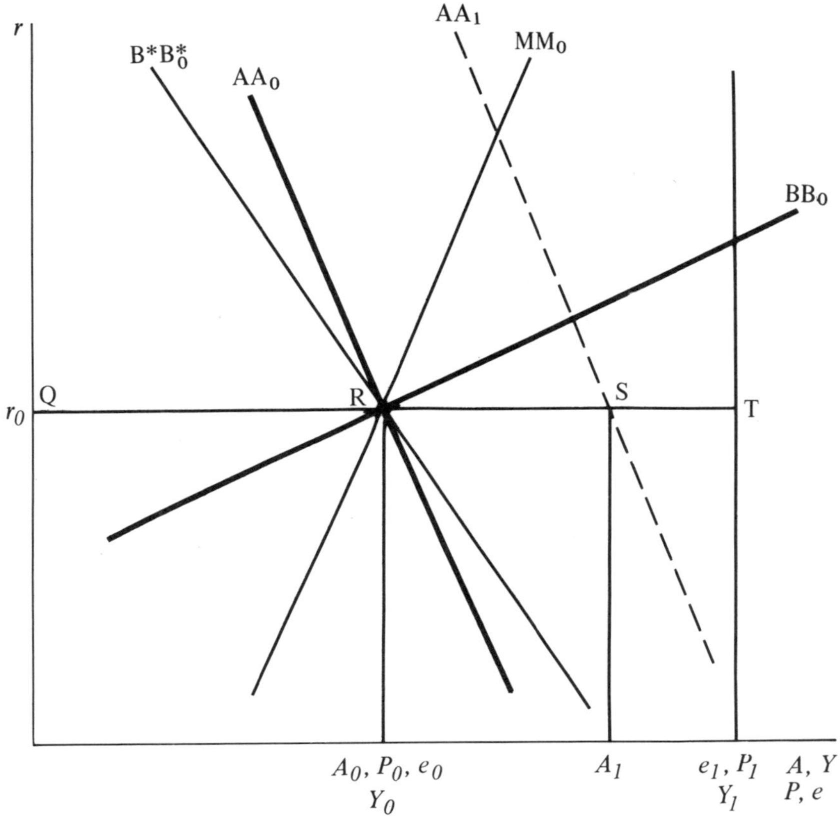

Figure 3-4. Devaluation and Adjustment in Absorption.

Second, the rise in the interest rate will raise the desired level of real wealth. Given absorption velocity, this requires a larger reduction in absorption than at the old level of desired real wealth in order to reach the new desired level of real wealth within the time span determined by absorption velocity. This influence is given by the second term in equation (3.19) which is also negative due to the negative sign. The two influences taken together determine the negative slope of the AA curve.

It is now possible to turn to the impact effect of a change in the exchange rate on the domestic interest rate. This impact effect incorporates portfolio equilibrium in the first period and at the same time points to the repercussions from the goods market on the interest rate.

The net effect of a devaluation on the domestic interest rate is obtained by first substituting equation (3.19) into equation (3.15) and then rearranging items:

$$\frac{dr}{de} = \left[\frac{1}{F_r^B + F_A^B \left\{ \left[(b^* - w) - \frac{\delta \bar{w}}{\delta r} \right] \frac{\delta \lambda}{\delta r} - \lambda \frac{\delta w}{\delta r} \right\}} \right]$$
$$\times \; [-F_A^B \, [\lambda w(F^{B^*} - 1) + a] - F^B F^{B^*}] \qquad (3.20)$$

From equation (3.20) a number of conclusions can be drawn with respect to the influence certain key parameters exert on the domestic interest rate. The rise in the domestic interest rate after a given rise in the exchange rate will be greater the larger the (negative) elasticity of demand for domestic bonds with respect to absorption. Stated differently, it will be greater the larger the substitutability between money and domestic bonds. As F_A^B rises, a given increase in the transactions demand for money due to an increase in nominal absorption will, to an increasing extent, be sought to be satisfied via sales of domestic bonds rather than via sales of other assets. Since, by the assumption of nontradability of domestic bonds, the stock of these bonds must be held by residents of the home country, their price will decline and their yield will increase more, the larger F_A^B. In terms of the schedules in figure 3-4, a larger F_A^B means a steeper slope of the BB line.

The rise in the domestic interest rate will also be greater the smaller the elasticity of the demand for domestic bonds with respect to their own rate, i.e., the smaller F_r^B. The excess supply of bonds due to a higher demand for money for transactions purposes can then be reduced only if r rises by a substantial amount. The smaller F_r^B is the steeper the BB line will be.

The overall effect of a variation in absorption on the interest rate can be decomposed into three separate influences. The first is given by the term

$$\lambda \, w \, (F^{B^*} - 1) + a$$

This term indicates that actual absorption will fall further below the initial level of absorption a the smaller the share of foreign bonds in domestic wealth F^{B^*}. The reason for this is that a small F^{B^*} leads to only a small increase in nominal wealth as a result of the devaluation. Therefore, there will be only a minor compensating influence on the decline in real wealth due to the rise in the general price level. Consequently, the smaller F^{B^*} the larger the decline in real wealth. At the same time it holds that the more real wealth declines the more absorption will decline. It is also obvious that the more real absorption declines the smaller the demand for real balances for transactions purposes will be. As a result, the need to sell off bonds diminishes and the rise in the domestic interest rate will be only modest.

The amount by which absorption falls short of its former level is given by the distance ST in figure 3-4. Note that in figure 3-4 the decline in absorption is measured in nominal terms at the new price level. The AA curve will be located more to the left the smaller the share of foreign bonds in total wealth F^{B*} and the larger absorption velocity λ.

There exists, however, an influence on the domestic interest rate stemming from the share of foreign bonds in wealth which is opposite to the one described above. This influence affects the location of the BB curve. It is given by the product $F^B F^{B*}$ in equation (3.20) and represents the (nominal) wealth effect on the domestic interest rate. The larger F^{B*} the smaller the rise in the interest rate from this influence. The explanation is straightforward. The larger F^{B*} the more nominal wealth will rise due to a devaluation. As a result, there will be a strong positive scale effect on the demand for all assets including domestic bonds. The larger the increase in demand for domestic bonds the more the price of domestic bonds will have to rise and the more the domestic interest rate will have to decline in order to equilibrate the market at a given supply.

It has been demonstrated above that the size of F^{B*} will have an influence on the equilibrium location of the BB curve. In figure 3-3 the BB curve will be located more to the right of R (S will be closer to T) the higher F^{B*} is. The rightward shift of the BB curve is due to the nominal wealth effect of a devaluation on the demand for assets. The more the BB curve shifts to the right the smaller the increase in the domestic interest rate.

A high share of foreign bonds in domestic wealth will hence tend to raise the domestic interest rate via the transactions demand effect and it will tend to lower the rate via the wealth effect.

A second effect on the interest rate stemming from a variation in absorption is due to a change in absorption velocity. Absorption velocity, in turn, is a function of the interest rate itself, as is witnessed by the expression $\delta\lambda/\delta r$ in equation (3.20). The larger the response of absorption velocity to a given change in the interest rate, the more absorption will decline, the smaller the transactions demand for money will be, and consequently the less the interest rate will have to rise in order to equilibrate the money market.

A last influence on the domestic interest rate concerns the change in desired wealth due to the rise in the domestic interest rate. It can be easily deduced from figure 2-7 that as desired wealth rises, absorption in any period of the adjustment process declines below the level otherwise affected. A decline in absorption, however, produces the negative effect on the interest rate via a reduced demand for money for transactions purposes.

The two latter negative effects on the interest rate find their expression in the slope of the AA curve. The larger $\delta\lambda/\delta r$ and $\delta\bar{w}/\delta r$ the flatter the AA curve will be. The flatter, however, the AA curve—given the location and slope of the BB curve—the smaller the rise in the interest rate.

First-period equilibrium after a devaluation is denoted by point Q in figure

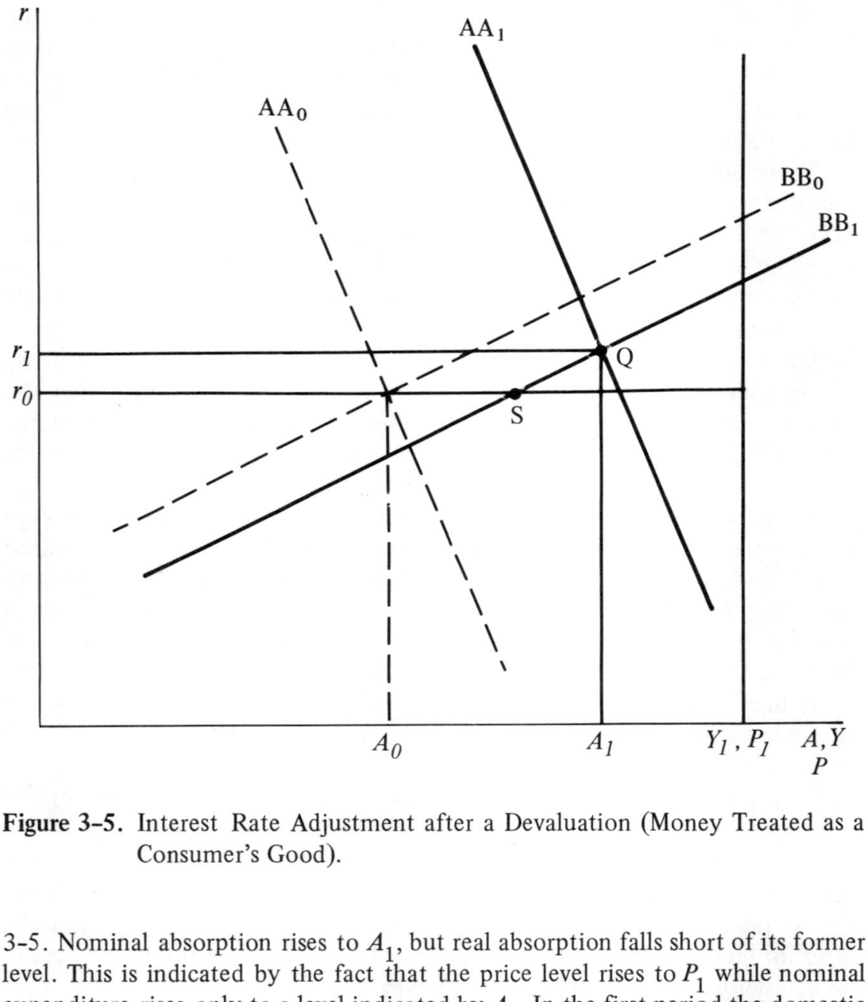

Figure 3-5. Interest Rate Adjustment after a Devaluation (Money Treated as a Consumer's Good).

3-5. Nominal absorption rises to A_1, but real absorption falls short of its former level. This is indicated by the fact that the price level rises to P_1 while nominal expenditure rises only to a level indicated by A_1. In the first period the domestic interest rate increases to r_1, a level at which first-period portfolio equilibrium is established.[19] The new supply and demand curves for money and foreign bonds (not drawn) intersect at point Q. The adjustment to point Q entails a capital account surplus due to the substitution of money and domestic bonds for foreign bonds.

Point Q represents an instantaneous equilibrium for the first period. It cannot be a full equilibrium point, however, since the nominal (and also the real) level of absorption A_1 falls short of the nominal (real) level of income Y_1. During the first period, the home country will thus accumulate a trade surplus equal to $Y_1 - A_1$ in nominal terms.[20] As a result, the stock of reserves will rise and the domestic money market will again be thrown into disequilibrium: the money market curve MM will shift to the right. At the same time, the increase in reserves raises the level of domestic wealth. Both effects require portfolio adjustment processes to bring about portfolio equilibrium. Domestic and foreign bonds are substituted for money. As a result, the capital account will go into a deficit.

As the portfolio is adjusted in response to the wealth effect of the balance-of-payments surplus, the BB curve shifts to the right of BB_1 and the new domestic bond curve compatible with second-period portfolio equilibrium is denoted by BB_2 in figure 3-6.

Apart from these portfolio adjustment effects, the rise in wealth also narrows the gap between actual and desired wealth and, thus, affects domestic absorption. Nominal expenditure will increase over the level of the previous

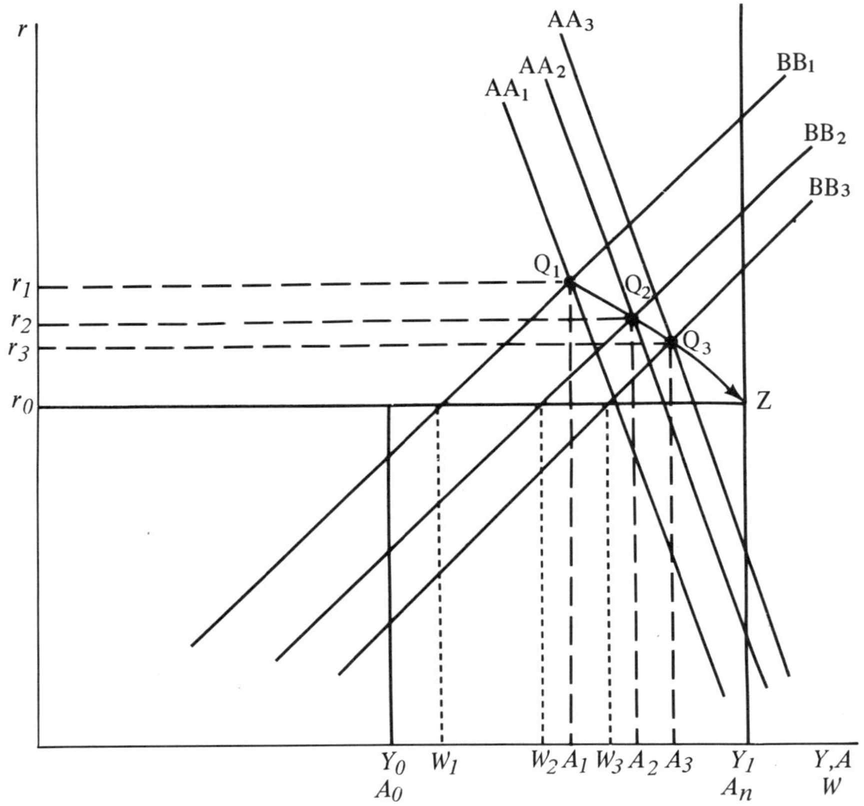

Figure 3-6. Portfolio Equilibrium, Spending, and Interest Rate Adjustment Over Time (Money Treated as a Consumer's Good).

period. The change in nominal absorption is indicated by the shift of the AA schedule from AA_1 to AA_2.

In the second period the equilibrium level of the domestic interest rate r_2 will be determined by the intersection of the domestic bond line BB_2 and the absorption line AA_2 at Q_2. Since absorption A_2 again falls short of nominal income Y_1, the home country will run another balance-of-trade surplus in the second period. Nominal wealth rises by the amount of this surplus $(Y_1 - A_2)$, and the portfolio and spending adjustment processes work as described above. The portfolio adjustment process involves now the (re-) purchase of foreign bonds by domestic residents. As a result, the capital account will go into a deficit. In the third period the domestic interest rate will decline to r_3 and the trade surplus to $Y_1 - A_3$. Eventually full equilibrium is reached at point Z where the domestic interest rate has returned to its predevaluation level.

At point Z nominal absorption equals nominal income so that the balance of payments is zero. Consequently, stock equilibrium obtains in addition to flow equilibrium: the country returns to the state of full equilibrium. During the process of adjustment, portfolio equilibrium obtains within each period and is disturbed over and over again by balance-of-trade surpluses which require further adjustment. At the end of the adjustment process the country will have accumulated an additional stock of reserves equal to the sum of the balance-of-payments surpluses. The nominal stock of money rises equiproportionally to the rate of depreciation of the home country's currency and of the rise in the domestic price level.

The above presentation has demonstrated the interaction between goods markets and various asset markets for the case of a devaluation of the currency of a small open economy. It pointed out that as long as the country is either a net creditor or a net debtor in foreign currency, a devaluation will produce a change in nominal wealth measured in domestic currency and will hence bring about a reshuffling of the portfolio due to the wealth effect. If at least some domestic assets in the portfolio are not perfectly substitutable for foreign assets, the domestic interest rate will—even in the small-country case—be free to move and can thus deviate from the "world interest rate" which is assumed to remain unaffected by the change in the exchange rate.

In addition to this wealth effect, a second influence on the domestic interest rate derives from the increased transactions demand for money as a result of the rise in prices after a devaluation. This change requires an additional reshuffling of the portfolio in order to bring about portfolio equilibrium. The ensuant adjustment in the domestic interest rate will affect the level of domestic spending as well as the income velocity of circulation.

These reactions on the part of the public must generally be expected to exercise an influence not only on the overall level but also on the structure of demand in commodity markets. In particular, any decline in the domestic demand for goods and services as a result of both the decline in real wealth and the rise in the domestic interest rate will bear the possibility of unemployment occurring in at least some industries. The change in a "monetary" variable, the exchange rate, hence, has the potential of generating "real" effects in the short run. The above analysis did not allow for a study of these impact effects, because by the small-country assumption any deficiency in domestic demand was assumed to be compensated by foreign demand. Depending on the country under review this assumption may or may not be realistic.

The rise in the domestic interest rate and the possible emergence of unemployment is more often than not considered by the authorities a threat to internal stability which requires intervention. If that is so, inflationary finance is a real possibility. Any policy which aims at lowering the interest rate and at fighting overall or sectoral unemployment will inevitably change the adjustment processes after a devaluation. The analysis of the authorities' behavior in response to variations in certain key indicators of economic performance requires less rigid assumptions than those made in this and in the preceding chapters. It will be taken up at a later stage of the study. The analysis in this chapter was exclusively intended to demonstrate various basic portfolio adjustment processes, their interaction with spending decisions and the development of the domestic interest rate over time until final full equilibrium is reattained. Adjustments in the real sector were considered only in passing; in the following chapter they will be examined in more detail.

4 Traded and Nontraded Goods in Devaluation Analysis

Adjustment after a Devaluation

Application of the Narrow Wealth Concept

The distinguishing feature in all previous chapters of the analysis has been the complete reliance on the real balance (real wealth) effect as the driving force of adjustment toward equilibrium after a devaluation. Devaluation was seen to raise the price level and thus, create a disequilibrium between actual and desired real balances. In the absence of any compensating increase in the domestic sources of the money stock generated by the domestic monetary authorities, the public adjusted spending behavior so as to acquire the desired money balances via temporary balance-of-payments surpluses from abroad. Factors other than the real balance effect, e.g., variations in the interest rate, were seen to affect the speed of adjustment but not the overall size of reserve accumulation. Because of the assumption that all goods were traded and that the country under review was a small country which faced given terms of trade, no relative price effect like the one expounded by the elasticity approach could take effect in the adjustment process after a devaluation.

The above assumptions in connection with perfect arbitrage also ensured that domestic prices adjusted immediately and fully to a change in the exchange rate so as to raise the domestic price level by the percentage of the devaluation. An extension of the model reintroduces a relative price effect into the analysis of a devaluation and, at the same time, abolishes the assumption of immediate and full adjustment of the domestic price level.

The extension emphasizes the distinction between traded and nontraded goods.[1] Nontraded goods are a class of commodities which have such high transport and transactions costs that they are neither exported nor imported.[2] A corollary to this fact is that for equilibrium to obtain, the markets for these goods must clear locally.

Assume now that the home country produces and consumes two classes of goods: traded goods T and nontraded goods N. Since the analysis maintains the small-country assumption, the terms of trade are constant, and importables and exportables can be lumped together in the class of traded goods, which is treated as a composite good. If at the same time changes in relative prices between groups of nontraded goods are excluded from the analysis, N can also be treated as a composite good. The only relevant relative price is then the relative price of nontraded in terms of traded goods, RPN.

Assume furthermore that the home country operates at full employment. Given the stock of resources and technology, the production possibilities of the home country are characterized by the transformation curve RR in figure 4-1. The transformation curve implies decreasing returns to scale. It can be readily demonstrated that under the usual assumptions the supply of each commodity depends on the relative price of the nontraded good, $RPN = P^N/P^T$. Assuming perfect arbitrage in the traded goods sector, i.e., assuming that $P^T = e \times P^{T*}$ always holds, and, finally, assuming for convenience that the foreign price of traded goods P^{T*} is unity, the relative price of the nontraded good is given by

$$RPN = P^N/e \tag{4.1}$$

The supply functions for the two commodities can then be expressed by

$$S^N = S^N\,(RPN) \qquad \text{with } S^N_{RPN} > 0 \tag{4.2}$$

$$S^T = S^T\,(RPN) \qquad \text{with } S^T_{RPN} < 0 \tag{4.3}$$

where the subscript indicates the argument of the first derivative.

The public's preferences are represented by a system of indifference curves. It is implicitly assumed that preferences are homothetic so that the preference system can be represented by a single indifference curve such as I_0 in figure 4-1.

The public divides total expenditure $A = a \times P$ on the two groups of commodities according to their relative price. Outlays on nontraded and traded goods are thus given by

$$P^N D^N = f(P^N/e)\,A \tag{4.4}$$

$$P^T D^T = [1 - f(P^N/e]\,A \tag{4.5}$$

Recall that by equation (2.8a) real absorption is equal to[3]

$$a = y + \lambda(M/P - k\,y)$$

Making use of this absorption function, equations (4.4) and (4.5) can be written as

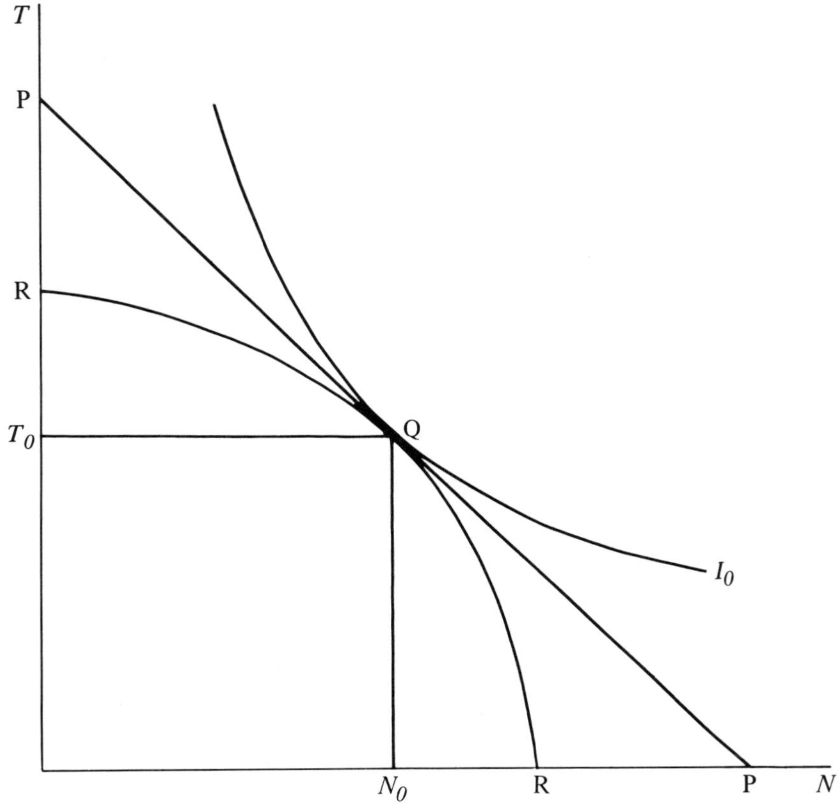

Figure 4–1. Optimality with Traded and Nontraded Goods.

$$P^N D^N = f(P^N/e) \times [y + \lambda(M/P - ky)]P \tag{4.6}$$

$$P^T D^T = [1 - f(P^N/e)] \times [y + \lambda(M/P - k\,y)]\ P \tag{4.7}$$

By assumption, y, k, and P are given at any point in time. The demand functions for the two commodities can then be expressed in their reduced form by

$$D^N = D^N(RPN, m) \quad \text{with } D^N_{RPN} < 0; D^N_m > 0 \tag{4.8}$$

$$D^T = D^T\ (RPN, m) \quad \text{with } D^T_{RPN} > 0; D^T_m > 0 \tag{4.9}$$

where $m = M/P$.

Equilibrium in the nontraded goods market obtains when

$$P^N S^N (RPN) - P^N D^N (RPN, m) = 0 \tag{4.10}$$

Equilibrium in the traded goods market defines external balance

$$P^T S^T (RPN) - P^T D^T (RPN, m) = 0 \tag{4.11}$$

Full-flow equilibrium, i.e., the simultaneous achievement of internal and external balance is given when both equations (4.10) and (4.11) hold. Full-flow equilibrium obtains at point Q in figure 4-1. The relative price of the nontraded good is given by the slope of the PP line. Total expenditure of the economy is defined by

$$A = a \times P = P^N D^N + P^T D^T \tag{4.12}$$

Total income of the economy is assumed to be equal to the value of output[4]

$$Y = y \times P = P^N S^N + P^T S^T \tag{4.13}$$

It is easily seen that any excess of income over expenditure is equal to the trade surplus provided that that the home goods market clears

$$B = Y - A = P^T (S^T - D^T) \tag{4.14}$$

It is noticed from equations (4.10) and (4.11) that apart from changes in the relative price of the nontraded good, changes in the money supply and/or in the price level will affect the equilibrium in the two respective markets. In the absence of sterilization operations of the central bank, changes in the money supply will be brought about by balance-of-payments disequilibria. Changes in the domestic price level are the result of variations in the price of either traded or nontraded goods.

Assume that the domestic price index is a linear homogeneous function of prices of nontraded and traded goods such that

$$P = \alpha P^N + (1 - \alpha) P^T \tag{4.15}$$

where α is the share of expenditure on nontraded goods in total expenditure. A rise in either price will raise the price level by that percentage times the share of outlays on that commodity in total nominal absorption. Any rise in the price level will, in turn, bring about a reduction in real balances and thus affect spending decisions.

Consider now a devaluation of the home country's currency. Assume that the economy is initially in full equilibrium, as indicated by point Q in figure 4-2.

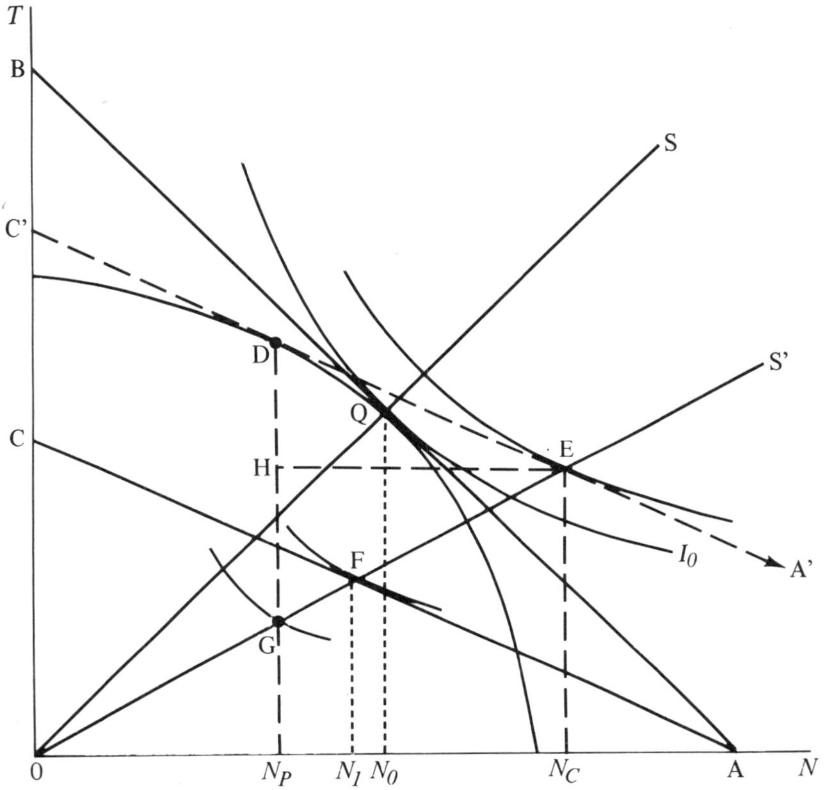

Figure 4-2. Devaluation and Disequilibrium in Traded and Nontraded Goods Markets.

At this point the domestic goods market clears and the actual level of real balances equals the desired level. Accordingly, expenditure equals income, net saving is zero, and the balance of trade is in equilibrium. The relative price of nontraded goods previous to the devaluation is given by the slope of the AB line. The AB line at the same time represents the budget constraint at constant prices. At point Q the price line is tangent to both the transformation curve and the indifference curve. Q thus reflects Pareto optimality in both production and consumption. At the predevaluation relative price, the public divides expenditure on traded and nontraded goods such that the composition of these goods in consumption is denoted by the ray OS, the "expenditure-consumption line."[5]

A devaluation of the home country's currency raises the domestic price of tradable goods by the percentage of the devaluation and thereby lowers the relative price of nontraded goods. The new relative price immediately after the devaluation is denoted by the slope of the AC line. This change in the relative price of nontraded goods causes substitution effects in both production and consumption.

On the production side the rise in traded goods prices induces a substitution toward traded and away from nontraded goods. If factors of production are perfectly mobile, the new production point will be located at point D. The value of output of the home country at that production point is described by the line A′C′. Provided all of the produced output can be sold at the prevailing prices, A′C′ also represents real income of the home country.[6]

On the consumption side the substitution effect causes a shift in demand toward nontraded goods and away from traded goods. The new preferred composition of consumption is indicated by the expenditure-consumption line OS′.

If all income that eventually accrues from production at point D could immediately be paid to consumers, the preferred consumption point would be marked by E. At point E there exists, however, an excess demand for nontraded goods equal to HE and an excess supply of traded goods—and thus an incipient trade surplus—of HD. Hence, E cannot be an equilibrium-consumption point of the economy. The divergent shifts in supply and demand as a result of the change in the relative price of nontraded goods will therefore induce adjustment processes which tend to bring about equilibrium in the commodity markets.

Apart from the above substitution effects on both demand and supply, a further immediate effect of the change in the exchange rate will work on spending decisions. It is the result of the reduction of actual real balances due to the instantaneous rise in the domestic price level. Given perfect arbitrage in traded goods, the domestic price level rises by[7]

$$dP = (1 - \alpha)\, de \tag{4.16}$$

As has been demonstrated in previous chapters, this rise in the price level disturbs the balance between actual and desired real balances and sets in motion an adjustment in absorption. Because of the assumption of homothetic preferences, both traded and nontraded goods will be affected equally; the demand for both commodities will therefore decline as a result of the reduction of real wealth.

The net impact result of the substitution effects in demand and supply and of the real balance effect on the equilibrium in the nontraded goods market is described by[8]

$$\frac{dEDN}{de} = (D^N_{RPN} - S^N_{RPN})\frac{dRPN}{de} + D^N_m \frac{dm}{de} \tag{4.17}$$

or alternatively, by

$$dEDN = [-(D^N_{RPN} - S^N_{RPN}) - MD^N_m (1 - \alpha)]\ de \qquad (4.18)$$

where *EDN* is the excess demand for nontraded goods.

The first term in parentheses in equation (4.18) summarizes the substitution effects in demand and supply, and the remaining term refers to the real balance effect. The two effects run counter to each other.

In figure 4-2, the substitution effect in demand is denoted by the movement from Q to E. As a result, the demand for nontraded goods increases from N_0 to N_C; the expenditure-consumption line shifts to OS′. The substitution effect in production leads to a shift of the production point from Q to D. Output of the nontraded good declines from N_0 to N_P. The net result of the two substitution effects is an excess demand for nontraded goods equal to $N_C - N_P$. Equation (4.18) indicates that the size of the excess demand depends on the elasticity of both demand for and supply of the nontraded good with respect to the relative price. Expressed differently, the size of the excess demand depends on the elasticity of substitution of nontraded for traded goods in both demand and supply. The larger the substitutability the larger the excess demand for nontraded goods in response to a devaluation.

The real balance effect of a devaluation on the equilibrium in the nontraded goods market is more difficult to trace in the above figure. If there is no change in velocity of circulation of money, if the entire stock of money is used for transactions purposes, and if, finally, there is no scope for borrowing from abroad, consumption cannot lie outside the new relative price line, AC. This line, at the same time, represents the real disposable income line in the sense that it measures the combinations of goods which can be bought with the existing stock of money after the devaluation. If consumers decide to spend all their income on goods in accordance with their preferences, the new desired consumption point—given the budget constraint—will be indicated by point F. At this point, demand for the nontraded good is equal to N_1. The real balance effect is thus seen to bring about a reduction in demand for nontraded goods from N_C to N_1, so that the total excess demand is reduced to $N_1 - N_P$. In the above case, D^N_m is equal to unity since demand is reduced proportionately to real disposable income which in turn varies linearly with the price level.

There exists, of course, the possibility that consumers decide to reduce their expenditure by more than their real balances have been reduced by the devaluation. In this case, D^N_m exceeds unity. Given the preferences of consumers, the consumption point will then move from F along the OS′ line toward the origin. The larger D^N_m the closer the final consumption point will lie to the origin. An increasing elasticity of demand for nontraded goods with respect to real balances will thus tend to reduce the excess demand for this good and could conceivably produce an excess supply.

The only point which is consistent with instantaneous equilibrium in the home goods market is indicated by G. At this point, there exists an excess supply of traded goods equal to DG. The small-country assumption implies an infinitely elastic demand for domestic traded goods by the rest of the world. Consequently, the excess supply of domestic traded goods will be fully absorbed by the rest of the world. This way a trade surplus of DG is generated which is equal in size to the excess of income over expenditure. The part DH of the total surplus is due to the substitution effect, and the part GH is the result of the real balance effect.

Equation (4.18) indicates that an immediate equilibrium requires a very specific constellation of supply and demand elasticities. Suppose that this constellation is not given, and, therefore, an excess demand for nontraded goods remains. Given price flexibility in the nontraded goods markets, this excess demand inevitably induces a rise in nontraded goods prices. This rise tends to reduce the initial fall in the relative price and brings about a second adjustment process in demand and supply.

The impact effect of a change in the exchange rate on the price of home goods is denoted by

$$dP^N = \frac{(S^N_{RPN} - D^N_{RPN}) - MD^N_m\,(1 - \alpha)}{(S^N_{RPN} - D^N_{RPN}) + MD^N_m\,\alpha}\,de \tag{4.19}$$

As in the above derivation of the excess demand for nontraded goods, there exist two separate and opposing influences on the price level of home goods. The substitution effect in production and consumption tends to increase prices, whereas the real balance effect tends to reduce prices.

The net impact effect of a devaluation on the price of home goods is ambiguous. If the sum of the two substitution effects is stronger than the real balance effect, i.e., if $(S^N_{RPN} - D^N_{RPN}) > MD^N_m\,(1 - \alpha)$, the price will rise and vice versa. If the two are equal, the price of home goods will remain unaffected in the first period, the relative price of home goods will unambiguously fall.

Equations (4.18) and (4.19) indicate that the strength of the real balance effect will depend on two factors: first, the weight of traded goods in the price index $(1 - \alpha)$. The larger this weight, the higher the instantaneous rise in the price level and, consequently, the larger the reduction in real balances. A strong reduction in real balances in turn leads to an important adjustment in overall demand. A high initial share of expenditure on traded goods in total expenditure will thus tend to reduce the upward pressure on the price of home goods via the real balance effect.

The strength of the real balance effect is also seen to depend on the responsiveness of demand for nontraded goods to differences between actual and desired real balances D^N_m. The greater this responsiveness the more important the decline in demand due to a given reduction in real balances, and, thus, the greater the chance that the positive substitution effect is cancelled by the real balance effect.

Assume, however, that the real balance effect does not outweigh the substitution effect, so that an excess demand for home goods persists. Assume in particular that D_m^N equals unity, so that the desired consumption point is given by point F in figure 4-3. The price of home goods will then rise by an amount given by equation (4.19). Figure 4-3 depicts the secondary adjustment process after the impact effect of a devaluation. The rise in nontraded goods prices lowers the demand for home goods on two accounts: first, because of the relative price and ensuing substitution effect; second, because of the real balance effect which is the result of the rise in the domestic price level by

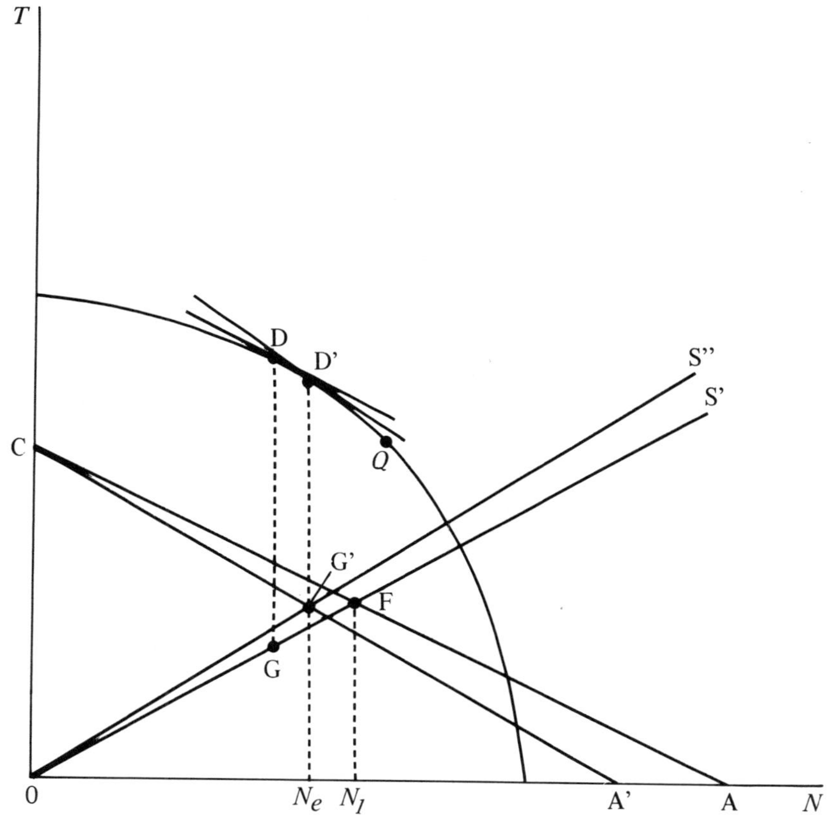

Figure 4-3. Effects of an Adjustment in the Price of Nontraded Goods.

$$dP = \alpha dP^N \tag{4.20}$$

The rise in the price of home goods shifts the relative price line from AC to A′C and the expenditure-consumption line from OS′ to OS″. In equilibrium, both demand for and supply of nontraded goods are at N_e. Due to the change in the relative price the production point moves from D to D′. As a result of this adjustment, the home country runs a trade surplus equal to D′G′ in the first period.[9] The size of the surplus after the adjustment in nontraded goods prices is denoted by

$$\begin{aligned} dB = (S^T_{RPN} - D^T_{RPN}) \times (dP^N - de) + MD^T_m \alpha dP^N \\ + M D^T_m (1 - \alpha) de \end{aligned} \tag{4.21}$$

Equation (4.21) indicates that the rise in the exchange rate—before any adjustment in home goods prices has taken place, i.e., at $dP^N = 0$—unambiguously improves the balance of trade. The ensuing rise in home goods prices, on the one hand, reduces the trade surplus via the substitution effect, and on the other hand, it raises the surplus via the real balance effect. If, on balance, the rise in the price of home goods is lower than the rise in the exchange rate, i.e., if the relative price of home goods falls, the trade balance will unambiguously improve.

The corresponding increase in reserves raises the domestic money supply. Real balances of the private sector will be replenished again and the private sector's demand in the next period will increase over the level of the previous period. This increase in demand creates an incipient excess demand for both traded and nontraded goods. Because of the small-country assumption, the price of traded goods remains fixed while the price of nontraded goods rises. This brings about a rise in the relative price of nontraded goods and an ensuing adjustment in the structure of supply as well as demand. The equilibrium supply of nontraded goods will be increased and the trade surplus will be reduced.

During the process of adjustment, equilibria in both the nontraded and the traded goods markets will be reached within each period. In the former markets adjustment is brought about by variations in the price of home goods. In the latter markets insufficient domestic demand will be complemented by foreign demand. Full equilibrium will, however, not be reached during the process of adjustment because the trade surplus which the home country incurs in each period and which results from differences between income and expenditure will jolt the money market again and again into disequilibrium. The ensuing adjustments in demand bring about disequilibria in the goods markets which require adjustments in the relative price and in the quantities produced in order to clear the home goods market.

A possible adjustment path for the system is illustrated in figure 4-4.[10] The

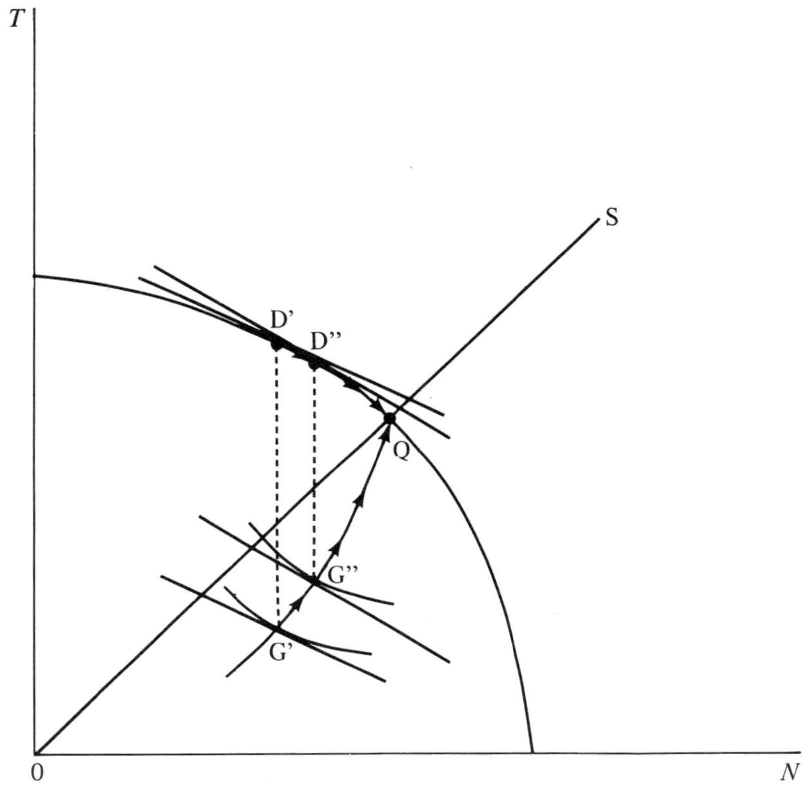

Figure 4-4. Paths of Adjustment in Production and Spending after a Devaluation.

position and shape of the G′G″Q line depends chiefly on the elasticities of demand for traded and nontraded goods with respect to the relative price of nontraded goods. If preferences are homothetic, the adjustment path for expenditure will have to lie below the expenditure-consumption line OS in the case of a devaluation and above in the case of a revaluation. The path for production will approach Q from above in the case of a devaluation and from below in the case of a revaluation.

In the long run, the system will restore equilibrium at point Q with no change in any real variable. In particular, the price of nontraded goods rises by the amount of the devaluation, so that the relative price returns to its former level. The corresponding rise in the domestic price level is supported by an equiproportionate increase in reserves and thus in the money supply. Actual real balances will again reach the level of desired real balances, and, hence, expenditure will be equal to income and the balance of payments will be zero. The system will be back to full equilibrium.

The distinction between traded and nontraded goods which reintroduces a relative price effect into the analysis of exchange-rate changes obviously does not impinge on the main finding of previous chapters, namely that a devaluation does not yield a permanent improvement in the balance of payments. Rather, it creates only transistory disequilibria in the money market and the goods markets and thereby in the balance between income and expenditure.

Application of the Enlarged Wealth Concept

The above presentation has relied on the simplest version of the absorption function in the determination of spending behavior. In so doing, it not only took a rather narrow view of what constitutes wealth in an economy, it also excluded variations of interest rates arising from shifts in the portfolio of assets, and therefore it prevented the analysis of the pertinent effects of these variations on spending behavior. The more complete version of the absorption function reads [equation (3.17)]

$$a = y + \lambda(r, n) \times [w - \bar{w}(r, r^*)]$$

The incorporation of the above absorption function into equations (4.4) and (4.5) requires that real-money balances be replaced by real wealth as an argument in the demand for traded and nontraded goods and that the interest rate be added as an additional factor.[11] This change yields the following reduced form demand functions

$$D^N = D^N (RPN, r, w)$$

$$\text{with } D^N_{RPN} < 0; D^N_r < 0; D^N_w > 0 \qquad (4.22)$$

$$D^T = D^T (RPN, r, w)$$

$$\text{with } D^T_{RPN} > 0; D^T_r < 0; D^T_w > 0 \qquad (4.23)$$

D^N_r incorporates both the effect of a change in the interest rate on desired wealth, and consequently on demand, and the effect on absorption velocity, and thus on demand, within a particular period.

The impact effect of a change in the exchange rate on the equilibrium in the market for nontraded goods is given by[12]

$$dEDN = \left\{ -(D^N_{RPN} - S^N_{RPN}) + D^N_r \frac{\delta r}{\delta e} + D^N_w \; [F^{B*} - (1 - \alpha)] \; w \right\} de \quad (4.24)$$

The equation distinguishes three influences on the size of the excess demand for nontraded goods. The first is the substitution effect. It is unambiguously positive. The second is the interest-rate effect. It is negative as long as the interest rate rises as a result of the devaluation. Whether the interest rate rises cannot be established a priori. The impact effect of a devaluation on the interest rate is denoted by

$$\frac{dr}{de} = \frac{-F_A^B\left\{\lambda w\,[F^{B^*} - (1 - \alpha)] + a\left[\alpha\frac{dP^N}{de} + (1 - \alpha)\right]\right\} - F^B F^{B^*}}{F_r^B + F_A^B\left\{\frac{\delta\lambda}{\delta r}\left[b^* - (1 - \alpha)w - \frac{\delta\bar{w}}{\delta r}\right] - \lambda\frac{\delta\bar{w}}{\delta r}\right\}} \qquad (4.25)$$

Equation (4.25) is directly comparable with equation (3.20) with the exception that instead of a full adjustment in the price level, there is only partial adjustment here due to the existence of nontraded goods.

The various influences on the behavior of the domestic interest rate have been discussed at length in the chapter on the portfolio adjustment processes after a devaluation. They are not repeated here. The influence of a reduced adjustment in the general domestic price level due to the existence of nontraded goods is not unambiguous. On the one hand, real wealth will be reduced by less than in the case in which all goods are traded. As a result, real absorption will decline by less. This keeps the transactions demand for money comparatively high and tends to raise r. On the other hand, a lower rise in prices results in a lower rise in the transactions demand for money, thus keeping r comparatively low.

The third influence on the excess demand for nontraded goods stems from the real wealth effect of a devaluation. It is clearly negative if the home country is a foreign debtor, i.e., if F^{B^*} is negative. If, on the other hand, the home country is an international lender, the wealth effect depends on the relation between the share of foreign assets in total wealth and the share of traded goods in total absorption. If both are equal, there will be no instantaneous change in real wealth; consequently, there will be no immediate wealth effect on the demand for nontraded goods. If, however, F^{B^*} exceeds $(1 - \alpha)$, the wealth effect will tend to increase the excess demand for both home goods and tradable goods, and vice versa.

It is important to notice, however, that even in the case of $F^{B^*} = (1 - \alpha)$, there will eventually be a wealth effect at work. This wealth effect will not follow directly from the rise in the exchange rate, but will rather be the result of the ensuing rise in the price of home goods. It has been demonstrated above that this rise in home goods prices will be the more important the larger the excess demand for these goods. Therefore, as long as home goods prices are flexible, the initial wealth effect of a devaluation will be complemented by a secondary wealth effect stemming from the induced rise in the price of nontraded goods.

The rise in the price of nontraded goods will contribute to the likelihood that the domestic interest rate will rise. The interest rate will, in this case unambiguously contribute to a decline in the excess demand for nontraded goods. It has been demonstrated above that the smaller the excess demand for home goods, the larger the trade surplus. The positive variation in the interest rate after a devaluation is thus seen to contribute to the desired adjustment in spending behavior and in the balance of payments.

In conclusion, it is observed that the incorporation of portfolio adjustment processes and the related variations in the domestic interest rate lead to an increase in the speed of adjustment via the dampening effect of a rise in the interest rate on demand.[13]

The incorporation of movements in the interest rate, however, neither changes the overall size of the accumulated balance-of-payments surpluses, i.e., the size of the change in the level of reserves, nor affects the properties of the final equilibrium position.

Adjustment under the Assumption of Official Intervention

The preceding analysis made the typical long-run assumptions of perfectly flexible prices and wages and unimpaired mobility of factors of production. These assumptions are not generally applicable to the short run and often not even to the medium run. The disequilibrium situations arising when one or more of these assumptions are changed may be of a substantially different nature than those described above. If at the same time it is true that policymakers feel compelled to intervene and stabilize the economy in the face of arising disequilibria in certain markets, it may be important to spell out which kind of disequilibria arise in the short run, in which markets they arise, and which policy actions may be expected to follow. Finally, one would be interested to know whether the actions likely to be taken by the authorities will rather tend to support or to undermine the desired effects of a devaluation.

Assume first that capital is specific to each industry and labor is immobile in the short run, but maintain the assumption of flexible nontraded goods prices. Assume, furthermore, that nominal wages are fixed over the period under consideration as a result of, say, a long-run wage contract. In this case, the supply of traded and nontraded goods is no longer a continuous function of relative prices. Rather the supply of each commodity is a one-sided function of its respective price. As the price rises, there exists an incentive to expand employment and output. Since, however, factors of production are immobile there will be no expansion of output: output and employment in each industry are inflexible in the upward direction. On the other hand, as the price of a commodity declines, the industry will incur losses because of the rigidity of labor costs. Producers will, therefore, reduce employment and output until the balance between marginal costs and marginal revenue is reattained. As a result of these considerations, the supply functions can be written

$$S^N = S^N (P^N) \tag{4.26}$$

$$S^T = S^T (P^T) \tag{4.27}$$

In the simple version of the absorption function (2.8a), the immediate excess demand for nontraded goods arising from a devaluation is denoted by

$$dEDN = \left[-D^N_{RPN} - S^N_{PN} \frac{\delta P^N}{\delta e} - MD^N_m (1 - \alpha) \right] de \tag{4.28}$$

This equation leaves the response of the price of home goods to be determined. The instantaneous change in the price of home goods is given by

$$dP^N = \frac{D^N_{RPN} + MD^N_m (1 - \alpha)}{(D^N_{RPN} - S^N_{PN}) - MD^N_m \alpha} de \tag{4.29}$$

The full impact effect of a devaluation on the equilibrium in the nontraded goods market–including the response of supply and demand to the adjustment in the price of home goods–is then denoted by

$$dEDN = \left\{ -D^N_{RPN} \left[1 + \frac{S^N_{PN}}{(D^N_{RPN} - S^N_{PN}) - MD^N_m \alpha} \right] - MD^N_m (1 - \alpha) \left[1 - \frac{S^N_{PN}}{(D^N_{RPN} - S^N_{PN}) - MD^N_m \alpha} \right] \right\} de \tag{4.30}$$

The excess demand for nontraded goods is seen to, first, depend positively on the elasticity of substitution of nontraded for traded goods in consumption. In other words, it depends positively on the responsiveness of demand for nontraded goods with respect to the relative price D^N_{RPN}.

Equation (4.30) suggests, furthermore, that *EDN* will decline as the responsiveness of demand for nontraded goods with respect to changes in real balance D^N_m increase.

Finally, the excess demand for nontraded goods depends negatively on the responsiveness of supply with respect to a change in the price of home goods S^N_{PN}. A large S^N_{PN} will tend to weaken the positive substitution effect in demand and magnify the negative real balance effect. It is therefore possible that a high elasticity of supply with respect to the price of home goods in combination with a given relative influence of the substitution and real balance effect leads to an initial excess supply rather than an excess demand for home goods. As the price for home goods falls in response to the excess supply, the supply of home goods will be lowered and equilibrium will eventually be reached at a lower level of demand for and supply of home goods. It is obvious from this discussion that unemployment in the nontraded goods industry is a real possibility.

A first-period equilibrium situation with unemployment in the nontraded goods industry is depicted in figure 4-5. Initial equilibrium is given at point Q, output and consumption of nontraded goods are at N_0. The production point after the devaluation is denoted by B, while the composition of domestic consumption is indicated by point A. Despite the rise in the absolute and in the relative price of traded goods, the production of traded goods remains unchanged at T_0 because of the short-term immobility of labor. The production of home goods declines to N_1 in response to the shortfall in demand and the ensuing fall in the price of home goods which makes it unprofitable to produce at the old level. The production point B lies inside the production-possibility curve. The horizontal distance between B and the production-possibility curve expresses the degree of unemployment of existing resources. The home country will, nonetheless, run a trade-balance surplus equal to AB. It is observed, however, that this surplus is significantly smaller than the surplus that would have been achieved if, in the short run, factors of production were mobile between industries. The size of the surplus in this latter case is given by AC.

Factor immobility and downward rigidity of factor prices is thus seen to have two negative effects for an economy. First, it bears the danger of unemployment arising from a devaluation even in the face of perfectly elastic foreign demand for domestic tradable goods. Second, it tends to reduce severely the initial positive effects of a devaluation on the trade balance. The speed of adjustment toward full equilibrium will therefore be largely reduced. In the extreme case, the improvement in the trade balance may be negligible, and, therefore, a devaluation may be valued as being ineffective with respect to the desired improvement in the balance of payments and as conducive to unemployment.

If unemployment arises from such a situation, it is likely that the authorities will react to this undesirable development. In order to cope with the unemployment problem, they may decide to introduce either an expansionary monetary policy in the form of an expansion of the money supply or an expansionary fiscal policy in the form of a cut in taxes. Both measures are expected to eventually stimulate demand and thus reduce unemployment.

Assume that the monetary authorities decide to raise the money supply. At given prices the rise in the money supply increases potential real demand. This can be represented in the graphs by an outward shift of the relative price line or budget constraint. In countries in which interest rates are free to adjust, the rise in the money supply will lower interest rates. As demonstrated in chapter 3, a fall in interest rates raises domestic absorption on two accounts. First, it lowers desired real wealth and thereby lowers saving. Second, it lowers absorption

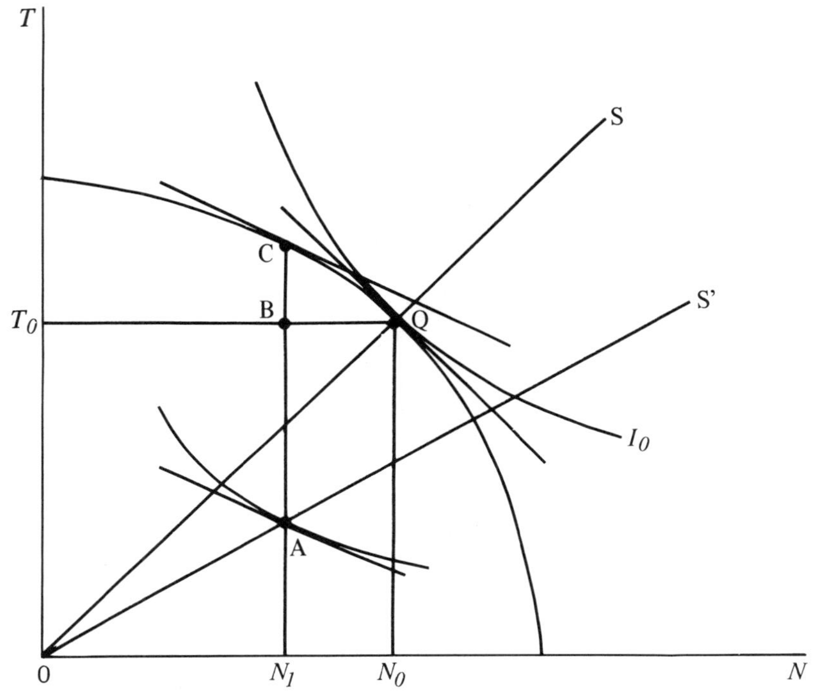

Figure 4-5. Devaluation, Factor Immobility, and Unemployment.

velocity since a decline in the interest rate affects the desired intertemporal distribution of expenditure in favor of present consumption.

At a constant relative price of home goods the increase in domestic demand is demonstrated by an outward movement of the initial consumption point A along the OS′ line in figure 4-5. As demand rises producers of domestic goods can raise the price for their produce. As the production of home goods becomes again more profitable, output will be increased and unemployment will decline. A situation in which the money supply is expanded so that unemployment is cut to half its former level is demonstrated in figure 4-6.

Initial demand after the devaluation is at point A, initial supply at point B. The degree of unemployment is measured by the distance BQ. The expansionary monetary policy increases demand and shifts the desired consumption point away from the origin. The absolute and relative price of home goods rises. The new desired pattern of demand is indicated by the ray OS″. The desired consumption point after the expansionary monetary policy lies at point E. The production point which meets that demand is marked by point D. It is readily observed that the expansion of the money supply reduces unemployment to DQ. At the same time, it severely reduces the trade-account surplus from AB to DE.

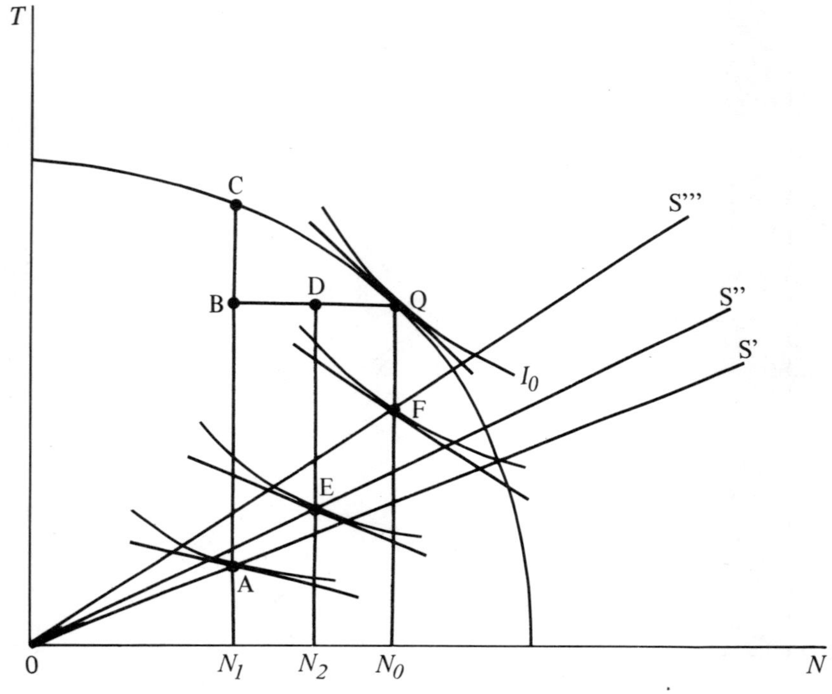

Figure 4–6. Factor Immobility and the Effects of Official Intervention on Production, Consumption, and the Trade Balance.

A monetary policy which wipes out altogether existing unemployment is indicated by the consumption point F and the production point Q. The trade-account surplus is further reduced. This observation leads to the general proposition that an expansionary monetary policy which accompanies a devaluation will tend to reduce the positive effects of a devaluation on the balance of payments, and will, thus, reduce the overall accumulation of reserves. By its intervention the central bank does not influence the final equilibrium situation, but it does, for the above reason, determine the percentage of the domestic money supply which is ultimately backed by international reserves rather than by domestic assets.

The fact that, in spite of its expansionary policy, the home country runs a trade-account surplus at all is a result of the existence of long-term wage contracts which fix nominal wages over the period under consideration. By this assumption real incomes of workers are effectively reduced after a devaluation. Consequently, aggregate domestic demand falls short of the value of output: the trade account improves. It is observed that the balance of payments improves at the expense of real incomes of workers. During the process of adjustment after a devaluation, the income distribution is changed in favor of producers (recipients of capital income) whose nominal income increases along with the increase in the value of output, while, at the same time, nominal incomes of workers remain unchanged; real incomes decline as a result of the rise in prices.

5 The Importance of Money Illusion for the Adjustment Process

Money Illusion, Wage Demands, and Adjustment

The previous chapter stressed the importance of intervention policies of the domestic monetary authorities for the path of adjustment and for the size of reserve accumulation in response to a devaluation. Monetary policies intended to stabilize certain key variables were seen to crucially affect the success of a devaluation. This observation can be strengthened and elaborated by presenting examples which stress the importance and influence of the existence or absence of money illusion for the success of a devaluation.

Assume that workers are not subject to money illusion and adjust their nominal wage demands in accordance with (upward) movements in the general price level in order to keep their real incomes intact. In this case, a devaluation which leads to an immediate rise in the domestic price level by $dP = (1 - \alpha)\, de$ will trigger wage demands of an equiproportionate amount. The rise in wages by that percentage will affect the two industries in different ways. In the traded goods industry, the rise in costs falls short of the rise in the price of its produce. As a result the return to capital in this industry rises, and there exists an incentive to expand production. In the nontraded goods industry, on the other hand, the rise in costs introduces prospective losses if prices are kept at their present level. Assume that the producers of nontraded goods decide to raise their prices by the percentage of the increase in the wage rate, rather than to adjust output.[1] This policy results in a further increase in the domestic price level and consequently in additional wage demands.

Given the above behavior of workers with respect to wage demands and the behavior of producers with respect to price determination, the first-period equilibrium will be characterized by an equiproportionate increase in all prices and wages. It is obvious that if wage and price increases are not monetized by the central bank, real balances of the economy will be reduced. This reduction, in turn, will have real effects.

In figure 5-1, initial equilibrium is again denoted by point Q. The equiproportionate rise in all prices will leave the relative price of nontraded goods unaffected. The rise in the general price level reduces real balances and aggregate

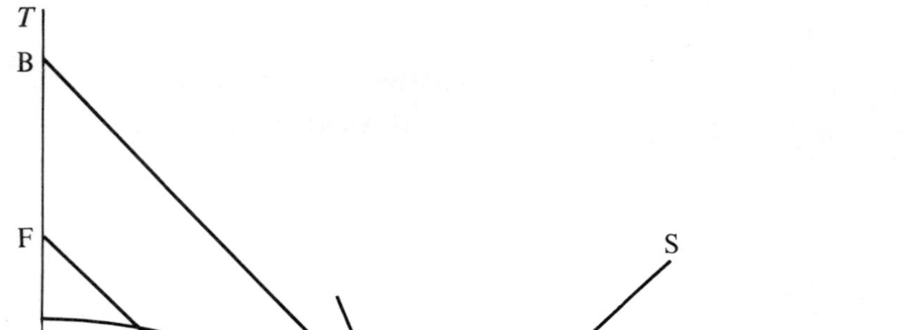

Figure 5-1. Production, Spending, and Trade Surplus in the Absence of Money Illusion.

real disposable income by the percentage of the devaluation. Whereas before the devaluation the combinations of commodities which could be financed with the given money supply at an unchanged velocity of circulation were given by the AB line, the corresponding combinations after the devaluation and the ensuing adjustments in prices are denoted by the CD line. Assume for simplicity that the responsiveness of demand with respect to variations in real balances is equal to unity ($D_m^N = D_m^T = 1$). The consumption point must then lie on the CD line.

Given homothetic preferences and an unchanged relative price of nontraded goods, the amount of real consumption that can be financed by the reduced level of real balances and which reflects consumer preferences between traded and nontraded goods is given by point U. At this point, demand for nontraded goods falls short of its initial supply by $N_0 - N_1$.

Since the demand for nontraded goods fails to support the supply at N_0, producers of nontraded goods will reduce output and lay off workers.[2]

In the traded goods sector, on the other hand, the excess supply of traded goods which is equal to UR will be absorbed by demand from abroad which is infinitely elastic in the small-country case. Production of traded goods will, therefore, remain at its predevaluation level T_0. The resulting trade surplus of UR is equal to the difference between the (real) value of output which is denoted by the EF line and the (real) value of domestic expenditure which is represented by the CD line.

It should be noted that the first-period trade surplus from a devaluation in this situation falls substantially short of the surplus which is obtained in the full-employment case. The trade surplus incurred by the home country will increase the level of money balances and will eventually raise real balances to their former level. Over time the increase in money and real balances will raise effective demand for goods, and, thus, employment and output are gradually expanded.

During the process of adjustment the consumption point will move along the OS ray from U to Q, while the production point will move from R to Q. Until final equilibrium is reestablished at Q, expenditure will fall short of the value of output, thus leading to balance of payments surpluses. In the case presented here, as in previous analyses, a devaluation does not bring about a permanent change in any real variable. During the process of adjustment, however, an important real change consists of both the existence of unemployment and a reduced level of real income.

Assume, however, that the government is alarmed by the emerging unemployment and decides to stimulate demand via expansionary fiscal and/or monetary policy measures. It is obvious from figure 5-1 that if these measures bring real disposable income back to its initial level in order to eliminate altogether the threat of unemployment, there will be absolutely no change in the balance of payments: the devaluation will not even have a temporary grip on real variables.

It may be concluded, therefore, that in the absence of money illusion on the part of workers, workers will press for higher wages which can be financed at full employment only if the money supply is increased. If, indeed, the monetary authorities decide to raise the money supply, there exists a danger that a devaluation may not work at all.

On the other hand, if money illusion exists, the effects of the rise in domestic prices will remain unnoticed. As a result workers will not realize that their real-income position has deteriorated and, consequently, there will be no compensating wage demands. At a lower level of real income, real expenditure is expected to fall short of its former level, thereby opening a wedge between the value of output and expenditure. Given perfectly elastic foreign demand for domestic products, the trade-account surplus will equal the difference between the value of output and expenditure; thus the devaluation will be successful.

Money Illusion and Spending

The result obtained in the previous section corresponds entirely with the view often held that money illusion is "a prerequisite for the efficacy of exchange rate adjustment."[3] The above presentation indicates, however, that this statement has to be qualified. The absence of money illusion is a necessary but not a sufficient condition for the failure of a devaluation to produce an increase in reserves via temporary balance-of-payments surpluses. Further conditions are the power of workers, or trade unions who represent them, to influence money wage rates in response to a rise in the general price level. Finally, the monetary authorities must be prepared to finance higher money incomes via an expansion of the domestic sources of the money supply.

If the two former conditions are fulfilled but the central bank is not prepared to increase the domestic money supply, there will be balance-of-payments surpluses even in the face of the absence of money illusion and given the power of workers or unions to press for higher money wages. The improvement in the balance of payments can be attained, however, only at the cost of unemployment.[4]

It is observed that the above results depend on a kind of expenditure (absorption) function which deviates from the one used throughout this study. Real expenditure is, in the above case, linearly related to real incomes of workers. As real incomes of workers are reduced by the devaluation, and money illusion exists, real expenditure will decline equiproportionally. A process of "undesired" and unnoticed saving takes place. Given full-employment output, a devaluation thus drives a wedge between the value of output and expenditure. The result is a balance-of-trade surplus.

If, on the other hand, workers are not subject to money illusion, if, in addition, they succeed in pressing for higher money wages, and if, finally, the monetary authorities are prepared to finance higher wages, then real incomes of workers will not change. As a result, real expenditure will not change and there is, consequently, no room for an improvement in the trade balance.

A devaluation, if it is to succeed, has to drive a wedge between real expenditure and the real value of output. In the above model, money illusion is seen to be helpful in achieving this goal.

The application of the absorption function used thus far in this study leads to quite a different result. Recall that in its simplest form the absorption function is given by [equation (2.8a)]

$$a = y + \lambda (M/P - ky)$$

Given full-employment real output at the outset, a change in absorption required for a successful devaluation can be brought about only through a variation in the value of actual real balances. In this context it has to be remembered, however, that equation (2.8a) is a function describing the behavior of the public. Therefore, it may not be appropriate to incorporate the actual value of real balances in this equation. What has to be included is rather the real value as perceived by economic agents. In particular, not the actual price level should be measured in the behavioral equation but rather the price level as perceived by the public.

Suppose that a devaluation reduces the actual value of real balances by $dm = -(1 - \alpha)\, de$, but that economic agents underly money illusion. In this case they do not realize at all, or only in part, that the price level has risen and that, consequently, their real balance position has deteriorated. In the extreme case of money illusion, they come to believe that their actual level of real balances is still at the desired level. Consequently, they will not revise their spending decisions and they will demand the same quantities of goods as before. As a result a trade surplus will not arise initially.

It is obvious from the example that, in this case, money illusion is clearly detrimental to an improvement in the balance of payments.[5] This result contrasts sharply with the result obtained in chapter 5. In the approach presented in chapter 5, the existence of money illusion prevents higher wage demands and higher incomes of workers, and thus, effectively reduces real expenditure: the balance of trade improves. In the latter approach, the existence of money illusion leaves economic agents with the impression that their real wealth position has remained unchanged. If this impression exists it will prevent the necessary adjustment in real absorption, and consequently there is no change in the balance of trade.

Money Illusion, Private-Sector Behavior, and Intervention

The above two contradictory results require a more detailed and thorough investigation of money illusion in order to discover whether the existence of money illusion is more likely to be helpful or detrimental to the success of a devaluation. Consider, therefore, a devaluation of the home country's currency and, alternatively, the existence and absence of money illusion.

Assume, first, that domestic residents are subject to money illusion. A devaluation at the stroke of a pen raises the domestic price level. Since, however, domestic economic agents are subject to money illusion, the effects of the rise in prices on real income and the real value of wealth remain unnoticed, and, consequently, there will be neither an increase in wage demands nor a revision of spending decisions; thus the real demand for goods and services will not change.

Given the initial stock of money balances in the economy, the financing of an unchanged level of real absorption obviously implies an increase in the demand for nominal balances if prices have risen. The emerging excess demand for money tends to raise domestic interest rates. If the central bank steps in and raises the money supply in order to keep interest rates at their initial level, it effectively finances real absorption at its old level but at higher prices. No wedge will be driven between real absorption and real output. Therefore, the effects of a devaluation will be entirely offset by an expansionary monetary policy.

Suppose, however, that the monetary authorities do not step in to control the domestic interest rate. The rise in the interest rate will then bring about either or both of the two following adjustments: First, the velocity of circulation of money will rise, increasing the "effective real money supply." Second, the rise in the domestic interest rate will attract foreign capital which, in turn, will meet the domestic excess demand for money. The capital account will report a surplus. Hence, though there will be no immediate improvement in the trade balance, the balance of payments will improve due to the capital-account surplus.

The process of borrowing abroad by domestic residents involves an exchange of interest-bearing assets (foreign or domestic debt instruments) for a non-interest-bearing asset (money) which residents require in order to finance an unchanged level of real absorption. This exchange will result in a permanent flow of interest payments to the rest of the world which will lower real permanent income and thus real wealth of the home country.[6] The flow of interest payments will produce a permanent service-account deficit which will be matched by a trade-account surplus.

Though subject to money illusion, domestic economic agents may not be insensitive to a reduction of their real incomes due to permanent interest payments abroad. These interest payments induce trade surpluses of equal size which absorb a part of national output. Economic agents may also be sensitive to the inconvenience brought about by the rise in the velocity of circulation of money which effectively reduces their welfare. Hence, even if they are initially subject to money illusion, economic agents will come to realize sooner or later that a devaluation tends to reduce their real income, wealth, and welfare, and they will engage in the appropriate steps in order to regain their former equilibrium position.

In the case of the absence of money illusion, individuals will immediately be aware of the deterioration of their real income and wealth position. Therefore, they will be confronted much earlier with the fundamental choice they will have to make in the face of a devaluation. The choice is exactly the same in both the case of the presence of money illusion and the case of the absence of money illusion. The difference lies only in the time of realization of this choice. It is the decision of economic agents whether to accept the decline in their real income and wealth position and, consequently, whether to engage in a deliberate saving process in order to return to the desired wealth position.

The absorption function used throughout this study implies that economic agents do realize the decline in their real wealth below the desired level and that in response to it they curtail absorption. They are not subject to money illusion; they do, however, either deliberately accept the decline in real income or else are unable to procure higher wages. This latter result obtains, for example, if there is perfect competition in the labor market, so that higher wage demands are doomed to fail. In either of the above situations the devaluation will be successful.

On the other hand, if economic agents are not prepared to accept a deterioration in their wealth position, and if the organization of the labor market is based on collective bargaining which enables labor to influence the price of its services,[7] then it will be up to the monetary authorities to determine whether the devaluation will be successful.

Though the final outcome of a devaluation does not appear to depend on the initial existence or absence of money illusion, the adjustment process will be different in the two cases. In the case of money illusion, there will be no immediate improvement in the trade balance since economic agents do not realize the decline in real wealth and seek to maintain the level of real consumption they are accustomed to. In this respect, money illusion impedes the desired adjustment in the balance of payments. There will, however, be a capital-balance surplus in the first and subsequent periods due to domestic borrowing from abroad. At the same time, the service account will go into deficit as a result of interest payments abroad. Later, as domestic residents fully realize the deterioration of their real income and wealth position, real expenditure will be reduced[8] and the trade balance will improve. The arising trade surpluses will be matched by capital-balance deficits as residents pay their external debt.

On the other hand, if economic agents are not subject to money illusion and if the central bank does not finance higher wages, unemployment will occur, aggregate real income of workers, and thus real expenditure, will decline,[9] and there will be an immediate improvement in the trade balance.

In summary, whether money illusion exists or not, the success of a devaluation depends predominantly on the behavior of the community with respect to wage demands and spending (or saving) once it has realized the deterioration of its real income and wealth position. In the case of absence of money illusion, the community will realize immediately that its real income and wealth position has deteriorated. In the case of the existence of money illusion, it will realize this fact only after a lag.

If, in either case, the public decides to deliberately cut down real consumption in order to regain the former wealth position, the devaluation will be successful. If, on the other hand, the public decides to press for higher incomes in order to be able to finance the former level of absorption, and if it is successful in this attempt, the success of a devaluation will depend on the decision of the monetary authorities about the expansion of the money supply, i.e., whether they decide to validate higher wage demands by an expansion of the domestic source component of the money supply.[10] These considerations indicate again that given the behavior of the public, it is above all the type of monetary policies of the authorities themselves which accompanies a devaluation which will determine the success of the devaluation.

6 Price Expectations and the Adjustment Process

Long-term Price Expectations and Spending Behavior

The previous chapter introduced the view that it is not actual price changes, and the accompanying actual changes in real wealth, that determine the spending behavior of the community, but rather changes in prices and real wealth as perceived by the community.

The various absorption functions used in this study thus far all implicitly assume that economic agents are free of money illusion. Furthermore, they assume that economic agents deliberately engage in a savings process after they perceive the decline in their actual wealth in order to regain their desired real-wealth position. It is obvious that this type of behavior is rational only if economic agents come to believe that the observed decline in real wealth is a permanent affair and not automatically corrected by some endogenous mechanism or exogenous intervention.

Suppose, for example, that economic agents consider the present rise in prices a temporary phenomenon and expect prices to return to their former level. As a result, they expect future real wealth to be exactly the same as before and thus to be equal to desired real wealth. Since wealth is not held for present liquidation but rather serves as a contingency reserve for a distant and uncertain future, and specifically as a reserve for the time of retirement, it is not the present level of real wealth which economic agents will compare with the desired real level, but rather the level expected to prevail at the expected time of liquidation. A corollary to this proposition is that spending behavior will not respond to the difference between actual and desired real wealth as observed today; rather it will respond to the difference between the level of real wealth which is expected to prevail at the time of liquidation and the desired level. It is, therefore, not the actual price level which will influence spending behavior under the "wealth motive," but rather the price level expected to hold in some distant future. If, therefore, as suggested above, economic agents consider present price rises a temporary phenomenon, there appears to be no reason why they should revise their spending decisions.[1]

Contrary to this type of behavior, it is suggested by the absorption function of the monetary approach used in this study that spending is reduced immediately after the rise in the domestic price level. The type of spending behavior which formed the basis of the adjustment process described in previous chapters, therefore, not only implied the absence of money illusion but also static long-run price expectations: the new price level after the devaluation was expected to prevail also in all relevant future periods. If the community holds static price expectations, it will consider a devaluation-induced price rise a permanent affair and, therefore, it will expect its real balances (real wealth) to fall permanently short of the desired level. There exists, hence, a rationale to engage in a saving process in order to reestablish the actual wealth at the desired level of real wealth. In the case of static expectations this "wealth effect" on spending, triggered by the devaluation, serves clearly as a stabilizing device. It is the key to the automaticity of adjustment after a devaluation.

The types of price expectations described above are only two out of a number of possible types which economic agents may hold. The former example implies an elasticity of expectations of zero: the present percentage rise in prices leaves the expected price unaffected. The latter example implies an elasticity of expectations of unity: the present percentage rise in prices leads to an equiproportionate rise in the expected price; the price level in the future is expected to be equal to the (increased) present price level.[2] If individuals expect prices to rise even beyond the level presently observed, the elasticity of expectations exceeds unity.

It is not at all clear on a priori grounds which type of expectations about future prices society should hold. There can, however, be no doubt that price expectations will be decisively influenced by past price performance as well as by the knowledge of economic agents concerning the adjustment process in an economy in response to a change in some important economic variable such as the exchange rate.

If past experience has been one of great price stability, individuals may consider the predevaluation price level as the long-term equilibrium level. They will, therefore, expect prices to eventually return to this level. In this case, the elasticity of expectations is zero, expected real wealth remains unaffected by the present rise in prices, and there will be no adjustment in spending decisions. If static price expectations are held, there will, therefore, be no immediate improvement in the trade account. The capital account will, however, report a surplus, because of capital inflows required to finance increased nominal expenditure.

In another case, past price performance might have taught individuals that prices are sticky in the downward direction: once they reach a certain level they do not return to their former level. In this case, economic agents might hold biased expectations: they are not sure about a possible further rise in the price level, but they know that it will not decline below the present level. Individuals then accept the present price level as a minimum level and their present level of real wealth as an upper value. Accordingly, they will engage in a saving process.

The devaluation will be successful in that it immediately improves the trade account.

If past experience is such that once an inflation gets underway it is likely to accelerate and thus drive the price level over and above the present level, the expected future value of real wealth will decline even below the presently perceived level. Accordingly, spending can be expected to be reduced even more than in the case of unity elasticity of expectations.

A further important aspect pertinent to the link between price expectations, expectations about the value of assets in the future and spending decisions is the degree of certainty with which expectations are held.[3] If experience with prices over the relevant period of time over which expectations about future prices are formed has been such that no clear-cut view about the movement in prices could emerge, individuals are rather likely to view the present price rise as an expression of a short-run fluctuation around a long-run, not clearly discernible, trend in the movement of prices. In this case, it is not rational to revise the view about future prices held before the rise in prices: the elasticity of expectations is, therefore, effectively zero. As a result, economic agents are likely to consider their real-wealth position as essentially undisturbed and they will, consequently, not alter their spending decisions.

Short-term Price Expectations and Spending Behavior

So far the investigation into the importance of price expectations has exclusively dealt with the real wealth or asset motive of spending decisions. This motive is based on the Fisherian proposition that spending decisions—or their counterpart, saving decisions—cannot be explained by present income alone but rather require a multiperiod approach. Saving is viewed as a process of wealth accumulation. Wealth, in turn, is accumulated for a number of reasons, all of which concern considerations of economic agents about their future well-being. The types of expectations relevant for the asset or wealth motive of spending are, therefore, above all concerned with the long run. Rather than the change in prices observed over the last period and the change expected for the next period, the price experience over a number of past periods and the price which is derived from this experience and which is expected to hold in some distant future determine spending under this motive.

There exists, however, also a short-run side to the relation between price expectations and spending decisions. Suppose that after a devaluation economic agents hold firm expectations about the long-run trend in prices. They will adjust their saving decisions in order to reach a level of real wealth which is compatible with their long-run preferences.

Suppose, moreover, that past experience has taught them that there are short-run, cyclical fluctuations of the general price level around a long-run trend or level. Let the expected value of the sum of deviations from the trend be zero. If such cyclical behavior of the price level is observed and expected to continue in the future, it is rational to adjust spending in accordance with short-run price expectations. This adjustment involves a substitution of expenditure over time,[4] as will be demonstrated below.

Assume now that prices start rising as a result of the devaluation and that the community expects them to rise even more in the near future. The expected rise in prices raises the expected capital losses on the stock of money held by the public.[5] It thereby raises the opportunity costs of holding money. The rate at which the community wants to accumulate cash declines. Economic agents desire to substitute real assets and commodities for money (financial assets). The expected rise in prices, at the same time, imposes a bonus on present consumption over future consumption. Both of these facts account for a hastening of purchases in the present period. The corresponding increase in demand may well be the reason for further increases in the price level. A part of the increase in prices will be financed by an increase in the velocity of circulation of money. An increase in the velocity of circulation appears to be a concomitant attribute of inflationary experience and expectations.[6]

The demand-determined rise in prices confirms previous expectations and leads to expectations about a further—possibly stronger—rise in prices. Expenditure will again be adjusted and cause, or support, further price rises in the next period with ensuing adjustments in price expectations. The more these expectations are confirmed by the actual development in prices, the more confident will economic agents feel about their expectations and the less doubts will they have about raising their expenditure in the present period in order to avoid higher prices in the next period. This way the possibility of a self-generating acceleration in the rate of inflation is not at all remote.[7]

If this type of spending behavior of the public exists,[8] it will obviously be destabilizing in that it raises absorption after a devaluation rather than reduces it. A devaluation, by raising the domestic price level, will then lead to a trade-account deficit in the first period(s) rather than the expected surplus.

Whether this development in the trade account will actually take place depends on the relative strength of the intertemporal distribution effect on spending compared to that of the wealth effect. Crucial to the strength of each effect is the kind, as well as the firmness, of expectations held about the long-run and short-run development in prices, respectively.

Price Expectations and the Dynamics of Adjustment

In order to study the overall impact effect of a devaluation on spending, as well as the development of spending over time and the stability of the system under various assumptions about long-run and short-run price expectations, it is necessary to modify the absorption functions which have been used so far in this study.

The incorporation of long-run price expectations is readily achieved. It requires the replacement in the absorption function of the actual price level P by the price level expected to hold in the long run P_{EL}. Instead of deflating nominal wealth by the actual price level, it is thus deflated by the price level expected to hold in some distant future. A corollary to this is that, in its decision about spending, the community compares the expected level of real wealth with the desired level rather than comparing the real level as perceived today with the desired level.

The incorporation of short-run expectations requires the addition to the absorption function of another term which expresses the specific type of short-run price expectations and the corresponding adjustment in spending. This term will reflect the elasticity of substitution of expenditure over time.

The combination of the two above expectation effects yields the following absorption function:[9]

$$a = y + \lambda \left(\frac{M}{P_{EL}} - \frac{L}{P} \right) + \beta \, (P_{ES} - P) \tag{6.1}$$

where P_{ES} is the price level expected for the next period.

Absorption in each individual period is thus seen to depend on long-term wealth considerations and short-term substitution considerations. As the expected long-term price level exceeds the initial one, the expected level of real balances M/P_{EL} falls short of the desired level L/P, and, as a result, the community cuts spending in order to approach the desired real balance position. On the other hand, as the price level expected for the next period P_{ES} exceeds the actual one, the community will hasten purchases in the present period and consequently, expenditure will be raised. Both λ and β are thus assigned positive signs.

In order to study the effects of a devaluation in a model which incorporates the above absorption function, various assumptions about price expections may be applied. Two of them are presented below.

Suppose, first, that past price experience indicates that the price level fluctuates around a rather stable value. In this case, the rise in prices due to the devaluation will not immediately lead to a revision of the formerly held view about the long-run price level; P_{EL}, therefore, remains constant.[10] Short-run price expectations, on the other hand, reflect the experience that, once a price rise gets started, it is likely to continue for a while. Short-run price expectations may, thus, be represented by the following equation:[11]

$$P_{ES} = P + \gamma \, (P - P_{-1}) \tag{6.2}$$

where P_{-1} is the price level in the previous period. The price level expected for the next period is seen to be equal to the price level observed at the present date plus a multiple of the increase in the price level over the last period. Depending on the elasticity of short-run expectations, γ may be smaller, larger or equal to unity. Transformation of equation (6.2) yields

$$P_{ES} - P = \gamma (P - P_{-1}) \tag{6.3}$$

Substitution of equation (6.3) into (6.1) yields

$$a = y + \lambda \left(\frac{M}{P_{EL}} - \frac{L}{P} \right) + \beta\gamma (P - P_{-1}) \tag{6.4}$$

Since by assumption the price level expected to obtain in the long run remains initially unaffected by the devaluation, the community considers its wealth position unchanged. Hence, there will be no adjustment in spending stemming from the wealth motive. On the other hand, the rise in prices over the last period leads to expectations of further increases during the next period. The magnitude of the expected price rise is $\gamma (P - P_{-1})$. The community will thus tend to hasten purchases in this period. The net result of the wealth and the substitution effect is positive: absorption will rise in response to a devaluation, the trade account will go into a deficit.

Notice that $(P - P_{-1})$ denotes the initial rise in prices due to the devaluation, dP/de. Hence, the first-period change in absorption is denoted by

$$\frac{da}{de} = \beta \gamma \frac{dP}{de} \tag{6.5}$$

Since β and γ are both positive, absorption will unambiguously rise in the first period. Absorption will rise more,

1. The greater the responsiveness of economic agents to a difference between the actual and the expected price, i.e. the larger β, the "price-absorption coefficient"
2. the greater the increase in the price level expected as a result of the increase observed during the previous period, in other words, the greater the elasticity of short-run price expectations; or expressed still differently, absorption will rise more the greater γ, the "price-expectations coefficient."

The increase in absorption will induce two important adjustments. On the one hand, it will tend to raise the actual price level. This will raise and justify expectations of a further increase in the price level and induce a further hastening of purchases. Absorption will consequently again exceed its predevaluation level.

On the other hand, the rise in real expenditure over real income will reduce wealth. Recall equation (2.32):

$$\frac{dM}{dt}\frac{1}{P} = y - a$$

Assume for simplicity that $P = 1$ initially. Real income y is constant. The first-period change in money balances (nominal wealth) due to the devaluation is, consequently, given by

$$\frac{d\left(\frac{dM}{dt}\right)}{de} = -\frac{da}{de} = -\beta\gamma\frac{dP}{de} \tag{6.6}$$

Wealth unambiguously declines as the home country finances the excess of real expenditure over real income out of its stock of assets.

It is obvious that even if as a result of stable long-run price expectations there is no initial wealth effect on spending, the reduction in nominal wealth will exert a negative influence on spending as of the second period.

In the second and all later periods, the wealth effect and the intertemporal distribution effect on spending will thus run counter to each other. It is not obvious on a priori grounds which of the two effects will be stronger as of the second period.

The exact impact on spending decisions will depend on the relative strength of the coefficient measuring absorption velocity compared with the product of the "price-absorption coefficient" β and the "price-expectations coefficient" γ. The decision-making process thus involves a difficult weighing of complex considerations reflecting various preferences and expectations.

At the same time the actual change in spending will depend on the actual decline in real (long-term expected) wealth in relation to desired real wealth. The larger this decline, the stronger will the wealth effect become. The change in spending will also depend on the actual change in the price level over the last period. The stronger the increase in the price level in the past period, the higher the price level expected for the coming period, and, consequently, the higher absorption in the present period.

If the net result of the two effects on expenditure is positive and absorption rises again in the second period, this will provide for an impetus for a further increase in the price level which, in turn, nourishes further price expectations. On the other hand, any additional excess of real expenditure over real income will reduce wealth even more and will thus drive an increasing wedge between actual and desired real wealth. The wealth effect on spending will, hence, tend to become stronger and stronger. The positive substitution effect will, therefore, meet with an ever-increasing negative wealth effect, and there will clearly be a tendency for spending to be eventually reduced.

As the wealth effect gains momentum, price increases will slow down. There may even be reductions in prices in a later phase of the adjustment, for there exists the possibility that price-expectations-induced spending has previously produced an overshooting of certain prices[12] and thereby driven the price level beyond its long-term equilibrium value. The intertemporal substitution effect will then work in the same direction as the wealth effect and thereby help to bring the system back into equilibrium.

The dynamics of the adjustment process is described by[13]

$$M(t) = \left(M_0 - kyP_{EL} + \frac{\beta\gamma P_{EL}}{\lambda} P - \frac{\beta\gamma P_{EL}}{\lambda} P_{-1}\right) \bar{e}^{-\frac{\lambda P}{P_{EL}} t}$$

$$+ kyP_{EL} - \frac{\beta\gamma P_{EL}}{\lambda} P + \frac{\beta\gamma P_{EL}}{\lambda} P_{-1} \qquad (6.7)$$

As t approaches infinity the first term of the equation approaches zero as long as the exponential term $\lambda P/P_{EL}$ is greater than zero. Since P and P_{EL} are positive numbers it will depend on the size of λ whether this is the case. As long as the difference between actual and desired real balances matters for spending behavior, λ will be greater than zero and, consequently, the first term will, indeed, approach zero. As a result (and due to the fact that in the long run $P_{-1} = P$ and, therefore, the two last terms cancel each other) the money supply will converge to its equilibrium value kyP_{EL} which is equal to the predevaluation money stock. Given that higher prices prevail after the devaluation, this fact implies that the equilibrium level of real wealth has declined.

There is no reason to assume that due to the devaluation the desired level of real wealth has changed. Therefore, the above result appears to be somewhat illogical and in contradiction to the reasoning advanced previously. The explanation for this deviation in results is to be found in the fact that the above derivation implies that the price level expected for the long run remains unaffected by the price experience over the entire period of adjustment. The value of real wealth expected to prevail in the long run is, therefore, equal to its desired level and there is no need for further saving.

The assumption of an unchanged expected level of real wealth throughout the process of adjustment after a devaluation implicit in the above derivation is defective on two accounts. First, given the price experience during the adjustment period it is irrational for economic agents not to revise expectations about the long-term equilibrium price level. It is rational rather to accept the equilibrium price level observed over the last periods as the long-term equilibrium level, i.e., $P_{EL} = P_n = e_1$. This upward revision creates a negative difference between actual (expected) and desired real wealth and thus initiates a saving process. Equilibrium nominal wealth is reached at $kye_1 = kyP_n$.

Second, suppose that despite the price experience in the recent past the community continues to hold the view that prices will return to their predevaluation level. Real absorption will then be at the predevaluation level, while real balances have declined due to the devaluation. The financing of the old level of real absorption at the new price level and a reduced level of real balances will, hence, require either the import of capital from abroad or a permanent increase in velocity. Both types of adjustment lower real wealth and/or welfare. The import of capital will lead to permanent interest payments abroad and will thus lower real disposable income and wealth. On the other hand, if the financing of the old level of absorption is effectuated by an increase in velocity of circulation, the rise in velocity will have to be permanent and will thus permanently lower the level of welfare via an increased inconvenience in financial activities.[14]

Both reasons, taken together or taken individually, will account for a revision of spending decisions and will ultimately lead to a rise in nominal balances in proportion to the rise in the domestic price level, thereby restoring the predevaluation real magnitudes.

Though the final equilibrium which is reached in the case of an incorporation of price expectations into the analysis of a devaluation does not deviate from the equilibrium attained in the case in which price expectations are neglected, the path of adjustment in the former case differs significantly from the path in the latter case. In the former case, there exists a strong probability of large cyclical oscillations in spending and in the level of real wealth. These oscillations may raise the feeling of insecurity about the stability of the economic system and thereby create inefficiencies in production, distribution, and consumption. As a result, the growth rate of output in the economy may decline temporarily.

If insecurity arises, it may, on the other hand, be helpful to the adjustment process after a devaluation. Insecurity may very well strengthen the contingency-reserve motive for saving. Under the influence of this motive, individuals will save in order to be prepared to meet unexpected losses in income and thus be able to maintain a given desired standard of living in the future. Hence, if accelerating inflation aggravates uncertainty about future real incomes, economic agents might decide to save more than previously.[15]

Taking into account the above arguments and derivations, one possible path of adjustment in money balances (nominal wealth) and in the balance of payments is depicted in solid lines in Figure 6-1. Another possible path is depicted in broken lines.[16]

Suppose now that economic agents have full information and perfect fore-

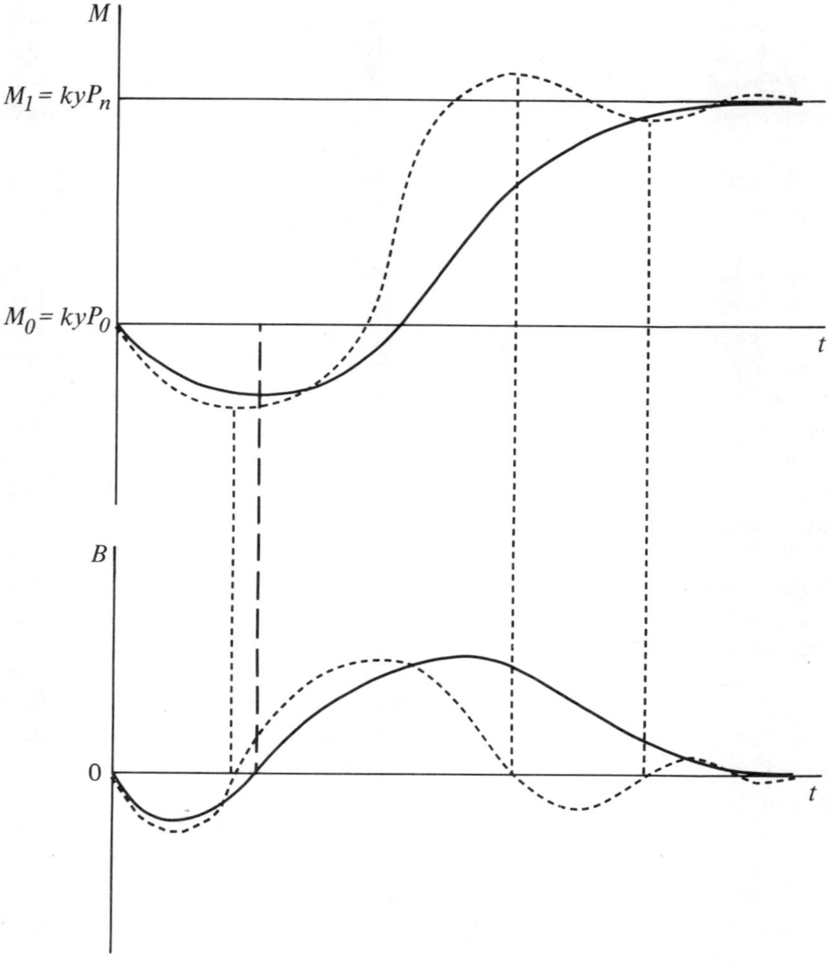

Figure 6-1. Adjustment in the Money Supply and the Balance of Payments with Alternative Assumptions about Short-run and Long-run Price Expectations.

sight. Suppose, moreover, that because of sluggish arbitrage prices do not adjust instantaneously. Let the domestic price level adjust proportionately to the discrepancy between the world price level and the domestic one.[17] The foreign price level (measured in domestic currency) after the devaluation is given by the new exchange rate e_1. Therefore,

$$\frac{dP}{dt} = \tau(e_1 - P) \tag{6.8}$$

where τ is the factor of proportionality. The domestic price level at any point of time is then given by

$$P(t) = (1 - \bar{e}^{-\tau t})\, e_1 \tag{6.9}$$

The assumption of full information and perfect foresight implies that the community correctly anticipates the rise in the domestic price level to its long-run equilibrium value e_1. Therefore, $P_{EL} = e_1$. Economic agents will at the same time correctly anticipate the price level in each of the next periods. Therefore,

$$P_{ES}(t) = (1 - \bar{e}^{-\tau(t+1)})\, e_1 \tag{6.10}$$

Substitution of equations (6.9) and (6.10) into equation (6.1) yields the solution for the dynamic adjustment of money balances.

$$M(t) = \left[M_0 - kye_1 + \frac{\beta e_1^2}{\lambda}(1 - \bar{e}^{-\tau(t+1)}) - \frac{\beta e_1^2}{\lambda}(1 - \bar{e}^{-\tau t}) \right] \bar{e}^{-\frac{\lambda P}{e_1} t} + kye_1 - \frac{\beta e_1^2}{\lambda}(1 - \bar{e}^{-\tau(t+1)}) + \frac{\beta e_1^2}{\lambda}(1 - \bar{e}^{-\tau t}) \tag{6.11}$$

As t approaches infinity the term in square brackets approaches zero as long as $\lambda P/e_1$ is greater than zero, which it is as long as absorption velocity λ exceeds zero. Another result of t approaching infinity is that the two last terms of the equation will cancel each other. This reflects the fact that close to final equilibrium the price level in the current and in the previous period will be (almost) equal. Over time $M(t)$ will thus approach its equilibrium value of $kye_1 = kyP_n$ which is exactly the same as in all other cases considered previously. Again, as in the previous example, a cyclical adjustment involving a decline in money balances in the first period(s) cannot be excluded altogether.

Whether a cyclical adjustment follows from the inclusion of the intertemporal distribution effect in the analysis or not, it is indisputable that this effect will tend to reduce the speed of adjustment. A corollary to this is that the stronger this effect, the smaller is the immediate reduction in real expenditure in response to a devaluation, and, consequently, the larger is the transactions demand for money. A rising transaction demand for money, in turn, raises the likelihood of a sharp increase in the domestic interest rate. The rise in the interest rate will often be regarded as a threat to internal stability, and it will be particularly undesirable if the devaluation was initially intended to cure existing unemployment. It is, therefore, likely that the central bank will pursue an expansionary monetary policy. The corresponding rise in the money supply, however, reduces the devaluation-induced difference between actual and desired wealth and thereby undermines the impact of the devaluation on the reduction in spending.

Apart from the above-described case of a defective anticipation of the long-term price level, there exists another possibility which can prevent the wealth effect from coming into play and from affecting spending decisions. Suppose that economic agents have had the experience that cost rises in the form of either increases in interest rates or increases in wages have always been validated by an expansionary monetary policy aimed at the preservation of full employment. In this case, the rise in the domestic price level—though fully perceived because of the absence of money illusion and though expected to continue in the future—will, in the extreme case, not produce any adjustment in spending via the wealth effect. The wealth effect will not be at work, because the community, in this case, anticipates an equiproportionate increase in the money supply in response to the rise in prices. The expected long-term level of real wealth remains unaffected despite the rise in prices. The wealth effect will not come into play. Only the intertemporal substitution effect will be at work. The trade account will, therefore, go into deficit. If economic agents succeed even in pressing for a compensation for the loss in wealth due to overspending, the balance of payments will accumulate a deficit rather than the expected surplus.

These examples demonstrate once again that domestic monetary policy measures which accompany a devaluation are crucial for its success. The examples also demonstrate that the price-expectations effect on the intertemporal distribution of expenditure tends to slow down the adjustment process and to give rise to important increases in the interest rate. The price-expectations effect may therefore add to the likelihood that central banks take expansionary measures in the periods after a devaluation and that the authorities thereby threaten the success of a devaluation.

7 Conclusions and Policy Implications

In the introductory chapter of this study, it was asserted that the exchange rate is a price of overriding importance. This assertion could be confirmed by the various analyses carried out in this study. It is, therefore, no surprise that the exchange rate figures prominently in the range of instruments available for economic policy. Economic history shows, however, that the use of the exchange rate as a policy instrument has often been based on inappropriate expectations as to the final results and as to the side effects of a change in the exchange rate.

Most frequently, a devaluation, for example, was expected to yield a permanent improvement in the competitive position of a country. It was, hence, expected to bring about a permanent increase in foreign demand for domestic products with a corresponding rise in employment. It was also, and above all, expected to lead to a permanent improvement in the balance of payments.

The present study demonstrates that this expectation is not based on solid grounds. In order to yield a permanent change in the balance of payments, a change in the exchange rate would have to either continually change the desired level of real wealth or, alternatively, effectuate a permanent change in the level of actual wealth. Neither of the two is likely to happen.

Desired real wealth, and in particular one of its central components, real balances, appears to be a fixed proportion of real income. If it is true that factor costs and prices are flexible and factors of production are mobile in the long run, then real income will develop along its full-employment growth path. There is no reason to assume that a once-and-for-all devaluation will have a lasting influence on real income. It is, therefore, not to be expected that the desired level of wealth will be changed permanently by a change in the exchange rate.

A permanent change in actual real wealth, on the other hand, requires continuous sterilizing operations by the central bank. A country which devalues its currency will sooner or later experience an improvement in its balance of payments. The related increase in foreign reserves will tend to expand the domestic money supply and will, thereby, increase the level of actual wealth. In order to keep the level of wealth at its reduced level after the devaluation, monetary authorities must sterilize the expansionary impact of the rise in foreign reserves by contractionary domestic monetary policy. This policy is obviously not feasible in the long run because the central bank will eventually exhaust its stock of domestic marketable assets and will, therefore, have to abandon its sterilizing operations.

A revaluating country, on the other hand, that continually attempts to sterilize the decline in the domestic nominal money supply will soon run out of foreign reserves and will then be forced to stop its intervention policy.

In summary, a once-and-for-all change in the exchange rate does not yield any permanent change in the balance of payments nor in any real variable in the economy.

Given the apparent preoccupation of politicians with short-run and medium-run economic problems, this result may not seem to be altogether discomforting to them. As long as the envisaged goals are reached over the politically important period of time, a change in the exchange rate may still be considered an important instrument in their tool kit.

Various analyses presented in this study indicate that, indeed, adjustment processes are set in motion which tend to produce the results which are generally expected from variations in the exchange rate. It has also been demonstrated, however, that a number of adjustment mechanisms can come into play which tend to considerably slow the adjustment toward full equilibrium. It is not unlikely, therefore, that expectations about the effectiveness of exchange-rate changes as a policy instrument are frustrated: the magnitude of the first-period changes in the balance of payments may be as disappointing as the actual variations in domestic target variables such as employment or the rate of inflation. Still, the analysis suggests that a change in the exchange rate will not fail to be effective in the long run.

The analysis demonstrates, on the other hand, that this statement cannot be made unconditionally. The success of a change in the exchange rate depends crucially on the economic policy measures which accompany it. The success of a devaluation, for example, stems from the fact that it reduces the value of actual real wealth below its desired level and thereby eventually induces an adjustment in spending. If, however, policy measures are introduced which partially or totally restore the former level of real wealth, no or only a reduced adjustment in spending will take place, and the success of a variation in the exchange rate will be undermined. In particular, a devaluation reduces actual real balances. If for any reason the money supply is expanded in response to variations in key variables caused by the devaluation, the initial imbalance in the money market will be reduced or even wiped out entirely. Therefore, only a reduced or no adjustment in portfolio allocation and spending will result from the devaluation.

It is obvious that these offsetting types of policy measures are, generally, not enacted by an arbitrary decision. Rather, they are the result of the authorities' view that adjustments in certain central economic variables will endanger the achievement of certain given policy objectives. The present study has pointed to adjustments in a number of central economic variables in response to changes in exchange rates. It is not unlikely that variations in certain of these variables will appear to endanger given policy objectives. Policymakers will have to realize this fact before making a decision about whether to change the exchange rate. To the extent that the policy objective which gives rise to a manipulation of the exchange rate is incompatible with other policy objectives, policymakers will have to decide whether, on the basis of their preference system a variation in the exchange rate is still a desirable and the most efficient means of achieving the respective policy objectives.

A decision of that importance is obviously often heavily influenced by political considerations and processes. The behavioral patterns of the public, the power of pressure groups, and the political demands and expectations of the electorate as a whole often lead policymakers to take steps in order to arrive at certain domestic policy goals which are not compatible with external equilibrium.

Suppose a country runs balance-of-payments deficits as a result of overspending. This situation calls for a devaluation in order to check domestic expenditure. Suppose, moreover, that domestic residents are not subject to money illusion and are decided and have the power to prevent cuts in their real incomes. If, at the same time, full employment is considered an undisputable objective in society, there exists an apparent conflict between the objective of full employment and the objective of balanced foreign accounts.

A devaluation reduces real incomes and real wealth and will trigger immediate demands for higher nominal incomes. If these demands are financed by monetary expansion, full employment can be maintained, but the imbalance in the foreign accounts will persist and possibly even grow. If they are not financed, temporary unemployment will arise. At the same time, however, the balance of payments will report surpluses throughout the process of adjustment toward equilibrium. It is not a priori clear whether the new equilibrium will involve balance-of-payments equilibrium. In order to achieve this goal on a permanent basis, the devaluation would have to change fundamentally aggregate spending behavior.

The devaluation of the pound sterling in 1971 may be indicative of a case in which monetary expansion went alongside a devaluation. Workers had obviously grasped the fact that a devaluation meant an immediate reduction of their real incomes in terms of foreign goods and a prospective reduction also in terms of domestic goods. Trade unions were eager and successful enough to press for higher wages. In addition, the government clearly decided to follow a full-employment policy. It, correspondingly, expanded the money supply by an amount which was considered appropriate to finance higher incomes at full employment. An additional reason for the expansion of the money supply was the apparent adherence of the Bank of England to a fixed interest-rate policy. For reasons which have been outlined in this study, the interest rate is likely to rise in response to a devaluation. Given a fixed interest-rate target, this situation clearly calls for an expansionary monetary policy. These two factors accounted for the complete failure of the devaluation of 1971.[1]

The relative success of the effective devaluation of the pound sterling in 1931/32, on the other hand, may be attributed to the fact that some of the above prerequisites for the failure of the devaluation in 1971 apparently did not hold in those years. First, there appears to have still existed an important degree of money illusion. Second, due to the high level of unemployment and to the much looser organization of trade unions, workers possessed much less leverage for pressing for higher wages in response to the cut in their real incomes. As a result, the Bank of England was virtually under no pressure to expand the money supply: the devaluation proved to be rather successful.[2]

The experience of the United Kingdom in the 1970s is indicative of another phenomenon related to exchange-rate changes, namely, price expectations. The pertinent chapters of this study pointed to the likelihood that cyclical fluctuations will follow exchange-rate variations if certain types of price expectations hold. In the end, however, the system was seen to return to a stable equilibrium. The models generally assumed that the central bank remained passive and did not vary the domestic-source component of the money supply. This may not be a valid assumption. If in expectation of price increases the short-run price-expectations motive for spending is stronger than the long-run wealth or saving motive, the community will raise aggregate real spending in response to a devaluation. As a result, assets will be depleted and it is to be expected that—rather than saving—individuals will first seek to restore the former level of wealth via demands for a compensation for the loss in wealth incurred during the time of overspending. In addition there may be demands for a compensation for actual and expected price rises. If, furthermore, short-run price expectations are highly elastic, the rise in prices expected by the public may easily exceed the rise in the exchange rate. Both factors may account for the possibility that the percentage increase in wage demands exceeds the percentage change in the exchange rate. If monetized, these wage demands will lead to an accelerating inflation, a further deterioration of the balance of payments, and a need for a further devaluation of the home country's currency. The home country may then enter a vicious cycle from which any escape will be very painful.

It is often asserted that a "devaluation is strictly equivalent to a reduction in the domestic real balances."[3] The present study suggests that this proposition is true with respect to the long-run results if, and only if, the same assumptions about the behavior of the public and the authorities can be made in both cases. The analysis advanced in this study suggests also, however, that making these same assumptions may not be realistic. In addition, it indicates that even if the long-run results are the same, the paths of adjustment after the two forms of disturbance will probably be different.

A devaluation raises the domestic price level and thereby induces expectations about future price rises. Since a devaluation is not an everyday event, there is little chance that people will have gone through a learning process which could have enabled them to correctly forecast the exact effects of a devaluation on the price level. It can, therefore, not be excluded that expectations about prices deviate strongly from the "normal" development of prices after a devaluation. The expected future price level may lie way beyond any "reasonable" level. The corresponding demands for increases in incomes will leave the authorities once again with the choice between either unemployment or inflation and balance-of-payments deficits.

On the other hand, a cut in the money supply creates, if anything, the expectation of a decline in economic activity. It must be assumed that the corresponding adjustments in behavior on the part of the public will be of a substantially different nature than in the case of a reduction of real balances due to a devaluation.

Though in the case of no intervention on the part of the authorities the final result must be expected to be the same in both cases, the differences in the immediate behavioral responses of the public will lead to different adjustments in important variables in the interrun and can therefore be assumed to induce different policy reactions in the two cases. If, unlike the usual assumption made in the monetary approach, the authorities do intervene, the overall effects of a devaluation will, of course, be different from the case of a cut in money balances.

In particular, a country which experiences chronic overspending and consequently continual balance-of-payments deficits may not be well advised to resort to a devaluation as a means to correct its balance-of-payments difficulties. There appears to be little justification for the belief that a devaluation will bring about the required change in spending behavior. To the contrary, as a result of price expectations and also since a devaluation is generally said to improve the competitive position of a country, no restriction in wage demands with the corresponding decline in real income and spending can be expected. The country will more likely than not enter a phase of runaway inflation.

A cut in the money supply, however, is likely to be regarded as a sign of a firm decision of the authorities not to settle with the excessive spending behavior of the public. It may, therefore, be a far more efficient means of achieving external balance under the above circumstances.

The existence of expectations in general, and of price expectations in particular, may be invoked as an argument for a managed floating system, rather than a system of freely fluctuating exchange rates. The line of thought could be as follows:

It is obvious that expectations which come close in precision to rational expectations can be formed only if variations in central economic variables such as the exchange rate do not follow an erratic random path. For rational expectations to be formed, it is, therefore, important that necessary adjustments in the exchange rate take the form of smooth and regular changes. This, in turn, requires that the central determinants of the balance of payments, and thus of the exchange rate, develop in a stable fashion or remain at their equilibrium level. In order to obtain a view about which way the exchange rate is likely to develop, it is, therefore, important to look into the stability of the determinants of the exchange rate.

It is often asserted that the private sector is inherently stable. This assertion applies to the behavior of private-sector demand as well as of its supply. The overall level of demand and its distribution over time and between various groups of commodities (traded versus nontraded) are a reflection of the preference pattern of the public. This pattern is believed to display a great amount of stability over time and not to show wild fluctuations which could result in unpredictable effects on the balance of payments. Gradual movements over time are, of course, possible and will affect the balance of payments. The supply of goods is also believed to follow a smooth rather than an erratic path, because it is hypothesized to depend on such variables as the supply of labor, capital, and the development of technology. All these are factors which are unlikely to display a jerky behavior. Again, as in the case of the factors determining private-sector demand, a trend movement in any of these variables will have an impact on the foreign accounts and, in a system of floating exchange rates, on the equilibrium exchange rate. The view that the private sector is inherently stable does not deny, of course, that there may be unexpected and important shocks to the system as a result of, e.g., natural catastrophies. Such shocks will generate violent, and possibly unpredictable, reactions on the part of the public. The resulting adjustments in spending and portfolio allocation can bring about sizable shifts in the foreign accounts and will thereby lead to important variations in the exchange rate in a system of freely fluctuating exchange rates.

Another potential source of imbalance is constituted by economic policy measures of the authorities which induce endogenous adjustments in private-sector demand and supply. To the extent that these policy measures follow an erratic and internationally ill-coordinated path, there will be irregular influences on the foreign accounts, and thereby on the exchange rates of those countries which are primarily involved because of their close economic links with each other. The unpredictability of these variations may give rise to "unsound" price and exchange-rate expectations. The corresponding adjustments in private-sector demand and supply may initially easily enforce imbalances created by the behavior of the authorities and thus add to the instability of the international financial system.

A recommendation which can be derived from this possible development, and one which is most frequently advanced, is, of course, that economic policy be internationally coordinated and set up in a way which is conducive to a stable development of international financial transactions.

Reality, however, is different. Individual countries are frequently observed to take discretionary and abrupt policy measures in order to stabilize their own economies. These measures will generally not remain without repercussions for their main trading partners and may, therefore, cause frictions in international trade and capital flows. For individual countries it may, therefore, be rational to introduce a system which allows for a regular ironing-out of erratic movements in the exchange rate caused by policies, shifts in preferences, and shocks in other countries. Exchange-rate expectations could, thereby, be stabilized and a stable behavior of private-sector demand and supply be fostered.

It should be noted in passing that if economic policy could be fully coordinated internationally, the question of the appropriate exchange-rate system would be largely irrelevant. Given, however, the experiences with international coordination of economic policies in the past and taking account of the above considerations, the question of which exchange-rate system is to be preferred over all others boils down to the question of which of the alternative systems is the least conducive to erratic variations in private-sector demand and supply and in the authorities' economic policy.[4]

The above argument in favor of the adoption of a managed floating system by those countries which are likely to be severely affected by policy measures introduced abroad has, of course, to be weighed against the likelihood and the importance of negative effects of a possible mishandling of the floating regime. An undesirable development in the foreign exchanges may arise from an intervention in the exchange markets even if there is no deliberate abuse of the possibilities which the system offers for exchange-rate interventions. One reason for an inappropriate intervention policy may lie in the great difficulties in correctly forecasting the long-run development of the exchange rate. These difficulties stem primarily from the apparent problems involved in distinguishing between short-run fluctuations in variables that affect the exchange rate and changes in their long-run trend. Recall also that for a valid forecast not only the relevant domestic developments will have to be anticipated, but also the developments in countries which are economically important for the home country. A major source of insecurity is again the lack of international coordination of economic policy measures which prevents almost totally correct forecasting. There exists, therefore, a great likelihood that inappropriate managing of the float may take place. If this happens it will generally be hard to correct without major adjustments in the real sector.

Suppose a country unintentionally intervenes in the foreign exchange markets so as to effectively keep the exchange rate at an undervalued level. This situation compares directly with a continual devaluation of the home country's currency. The analyses carried out in this study do not treat this case of continual variations in the exchange rate. Still, the description of the various disequilibria which arise from exchange-rate changes helps to identify the adjustment in central economic variables ensuing from a situation of persisting, and possibly rising, undervaluation of a currency.

In the asset markets, there will be a shift in demand toward money and away from both domestic and foreign assets. The domestic interest rate will tend to rise. This will attract foreign capital. Gradually, more and more ownership rights to domestic capital will be sold to the rest of the world. The private sector of the home country will have to transfer an increasing amount of interest payments to foreigners.

In the goods markets, private domestic demand will be continually held below the level of domestic output because the continual devaluation keeps the actual level of wealth below the desired level and thereby induces a saving process. The trade balance will be in surplus throughout the entire phase of undervaluation of the home country's currency. In a country in which price stability ranks high in the preference scale, the growing trade surplus may easily give rise to restrictive monetary and/or fiscal policy measures. These tend to aggravate the deviation of the actual from the normal and required development of the exchange rate. The effective rate of devaluation rises. A country may, thereby, easily get trapped in an inappropriate managing of the exchange rate.

There exists another reason why an inappropriate managing of the exchange rate over a certain period of time may be hard to reverse. The present study demonstrates that a devaluation produces a shift in the structure of production toward traded and away from nontraded goods. If the devaluation is a one-shot affair, this development will be gradually reversed. In this case, the shift in production may generally be expected to be effectuated by short-run adjustments in production techniques and ad hoc shifts in factor intensities. If, however, a country repeatedly depreciates its currency by an incorrect floating, the country's long-run pattern of investment will be distorted toward export and import-competing industries and away from domestic nontraded goods and service industries.[5] It is obvious that in this case a switch in intervention policies which would produce an appreciation of the domestic currency will be strictly opposed by industries in the traded goods sector, because such a policy would reduce the profitability of the existing capital stock in those industries. A reversal of the initial intervention policy may, therefore, prove to be politically quite difficult.

The arguments advanced in this study indicate that a country may be ill advised when keeping its exchange rate undervalued. In an attempt to replenish real balances the country will continue to sell property rights to domestic capital to the rest of the world and it will continually forego present consumption due to an enforced saving process. This latter argument, which appears to be detrimental at first sight, may, however, under certain circumstances prove to be beneficial for the country in the long run. If a country succeeds in keeping the value of its currency below its real value, this is a sign that it succeeds in avoiding a full compensation of workers for the decline in their real incomes due to the permanent devaluation.[6] This follows from the fact that if workers were fully compensated, the exchange-rate depreciation would be ineffective. At the same time, incomes of entrepreneurs rise by the full amount of the (continual) effective devaluation. The undervaluation of the domestic currency thus induces a redistribution of income from workers to entrepreneurs.

Most generally spoken, workers are consumers and entrepreneurs are investors. Therefore, if the fixing or managing of the exchange rate succeeds in keeping the domestic currency undervalued, it may bring about a shift in the allocation of production between consumption and investment goods in favor of investment goods. A sustained rise in a country's propensity to invest will, in turn, have an influence on the country's growth path and will, thereby, increase the potential for future consumption.

This point can also be supported by reference to another effect of a change in the exchange rate which has been outlined in this study. A devaluation was seen to produce a shift in production toward traded goods and away from nontraded goods. It is often asserted that productivity growth in those industries which represent the traded goods sector exceeds the growth in productivity in the nontraded goods industries. If this argument can be supported by evidence, and it seems as if it can be, then a sustained shift in production toward the traded goods industry will tend to raise the overall growth rate of a country and thereby improve its long-run perspectives for consumable income.

It is obvious that these potential positive effects of an intervention into the free determination of the exchange rate will have to be weighed against the negative effects presented above. An evaluation of this problem would go far beyond the scope of this study; in addition it would require an intimate knowledge of the preference system of the country concerned.

Whatever the outcome of a decision of a country about changing or not changing its exchange rate, it should be noted that a good many of the advantages which result from such a decision can be reaped by the individual country only at the expense of other countries.

There are, of course, exceptions to this rule. Consider again the two above examples. If an individual country's decision to devalue or keep its currency undervalued for some time leads to a rise in the average propensity to save on a world scale, the international community as a whole will benefit from higher future consumption as a result of increased investment today.

Or, for instance, if average productivity growth on a world scale can be increased by a shift of domestic production toward traded goods, again the international community as a whole will benefit from such a development.

Whether the effects of a unilateral decision about its exchange rate by one country will be beneficial to other countries or only for the home country will depend on the individual circumstances. It is clear, however, that such a decision will generally not remain without important consequences for a number of other countries. This fact makes it understandable that—as with any other price—there are at least two parties interested in the value and the development of the exchange rate as a price. Differences in the system of political and economic preferences between countries aggravate rather than facilitate the appropriate choice. In any case, single-handed decisions concerning the exchange rate that neglect entirely the interests of other countries may easily put a severe strain on the stability of the world monetary system and may have detrimental effects on the optimal allocation of resources on a world scale and all that this means for economic welfare.

The exchange rate is a price which is open to manipulation, but not free to be arbitrarily manipulated.

Notes

Chapter 1
Exchange-Rate Changes as a Policy Instrument

1. Mundell has cast the choice open to policymakers into the following statement: "There are two methods of bringing about equilibrium. One is to change the quantity of money, the flexible money or fixed exchange rate solution; the other is to change the price of money, the fixed money or flexible exchange rate solution." See Robert A. Mundell, *Monetary Theory: Inflation, Interest, and Growth in the World Economy* (Pacific Palisades, Calif.: Goodyear, 1971), p. 93.

2. The conditions for an improvement in the balance of trade found expression in the "Marshall-Lerner condition." Assuming infinite elasticities of supply, this condition requires that the sum of the elasticities of domestic demand for imports and foreign demand for domestic exports exceed unity in order to generate an improvement in the trade balance. The assumption of infinitely elastic supplies appeared to be justified during the periods of mass unemployment in the 1920s and early 1930s but could not easily be defended thereafter. The recognition of this fact led to a more general expression, the "Robinson-Metzler-Bikerdike condition," which allows for less-than-infinite supply elasticities.

3. See Sidney S. Alexander, "Effects of a Devaluation on a Trade Balance," IMF *Staff Papers,* 2, No. 2 (April 1952), pp. 263-278.

4. In his original article, Alexander concentrates on the trade balance and neglects adjustments in capital flows. Therefore, it is the trade balance rather than the balance of payments as a whole which is equal to the difference between income and expenditure.

5. The "monetary approach to the balance of payments" has its roots in the writings of Johnson, Mundell, Prais, Dornbusch, and others. See, e.g., Harry G. Johnson, "Towards a General Theory of the Balance of Payments," *International Trade and Economic Growth,* Harry G. Johnson, (London: Allen & Unwin, 1958); pp. 153-168; Harry G. Johnson, "The Monetary Approach to Balance of Payments Theory," *International Trade and Money,* ed. Michael B. Connolly and Alexander K. Swoboda (London: Allen & Unwin, 1973); pp. 206-224; Robert A. Mundell, *International Economics* (New York: Macmillan, 1968); Mundell, *Monetary Theory;* Rüdiger Dornbusch, "Devaluation, Money and Nontraded Goods," *American Economic Review,* 63 (1973), pp. 871-880; Rüdiger Dornbusch, "Currency Depreciation, Hoarding and Relative Prices, *Journal of Political Economy,* 81 (July/August 1973), pp. 893-915; S.J. Prais, "Some Mathematical Notes on the Quantity Theory of Money in an Open Economy," IMF *Staff Papers,* 8 (May 1961), pp. 212-226. For an

empirical analysis of Germany see Manfred Willms and Klaus Masuhr, "Zahlungsbilanz und Internationaler Monetärer Anpassungsprozess," unpublished manuscript, Institut für Wirtschaftspolitik, Kiel, 1976.

6. Compare G.C. Archibald and R.G. Lipsey, "Monetary and Value Theory: A Critique of Lange and Patinkin," *Review of Economic Studies,* 26 (October 1958), pp. 1-22.

7. An exception may be the case in which a country desires an increase in the level of its foreign reserves. It will be shown in this study that a devaluation is an appropriate policy measure to achieve this goal.

Chapter 2
Devaluation, Wealth, and Spending

1. This chapter draws heavily on the lucid summaries of the general principles which constitute the monetary approach to balance-of-payments analysis by Michael Mussa, "A Monetary Approach to Balance of Payments Analysis," *Journal of Money, Credit, and Banking,* 5, (August 1974), pp. 333-351, and Alexander K. Swoboda, "Monetary Approaches to Balance of Payments Theory: Framework for a Survey," *Recent Issues in International Monetary Economics,* ed. Emil M. Claassen and Pascal Salin (Amsterdam: North-Holland, 1976), pp. 3-23.

2. Mussa, "A Monetary Approach", p. 337.

3. The fact that the monetary approach concentrates on the explanation of changes in the official settlements balance rather than on the determinants of changes in the various subbalances does not bar an analysis of these balances during the adjustment process. See, for example, Jacob A. Frenkel and Carlos A. Rodriguez, "Portfolio Equilibrium and the Balance of Payments: A Monetary Approach," *American Economic Review,* 65 (September 1975), pp. 674-688. See also the last section of chapter 2.

4. For an analysis of the money-supply process see, e.g., Albert Burger, *The Money Supply Process* (Belmont, Calif.: Wadsworth, 1971); Karl Brunner and Allan H. Meltzer, "Some Further Investigations of Demand and Supply Functions of Money," *Journal of Finance,* 19, No. 2 Part 1 (May 1964), pp. 240-283; Jürgen Siebke and Manfred Willms, *Theorie der Geldpolitik* (Berlin, Heidelberg, New York: Springer, 1974). An analysis of the money-supply process in an open economy is provided by Karl Brunner, "Money Supply Process and Monetary Policy in an Open Economy," *International Trade and Money,* ed. Michael Connolly and Alexander K. Swoboda (London: Allen & Unwin, 1973), pp. 127-166; Manfred Willms, "Controlling Money in an Open Economy: The German Case," *Federal Reserve Bank of St. Louis Review* (April 1971), pp. 10-27.

5. Incidentally, this is the situation of the famous "liquidity trap" in Keynesian economics.

6. Milton Friedman, "The Quantity Theory of Money: A Restatement," *Studies in the Quantity Theory of Money,* ed. Milton Friedman (Chicago: University of Chicago Press, 1956), pp. 3-21.

7. See, e.g., Jürgen Siebke and Manfred Willms, "Das Geldangebot in der Bundesrepublik Deutschland. Eine empirische Analyse für die Periode 1958-1968," *Zeitschrift für die gesamte Staatswissenschaft,* 126 No. 1 (1970), pp. 55-74; Albert E. Burger, "The Relationship between Monetary Base and Money: How Close?" *Federal Reserve Bank of St. Louis Review,* October 1975, pp. 3-8.

8. See Alexander, "Effects of a Devaluation."

9. See, for example, Dornbusch, "Devaluation, Money and Nontraded Goods"; Rüdiger Dornbusch, "Real and Monetary Aspects of the Effects of Exchange Rate Changes," *National Monetary Policies and the International Financial System,* ed. Robert Z. Aliber (Chicago: University of Chicago Press, 1974), pp. 64-81; Michael Mussa, "Tariffs and the Balance of Payments: A Monetary Approach," *The Monetary Approach to the Balance of Payments,* ed. Jacob Frenkel and Harry G. Johnson (London: Allen & Unwin, 1976), pp. 187-221.

10. The concept of "absorption velocity" is identical to that of "consumption velocity" in Rüdiger Dornbusch and Michael Mussa, "Consumption, Real Balances and the Hoarding Function," *International Economic Review,* 16 (1975), pp. 415-421. Dornbusch and Mussa show that this form of a consumption (absorption) function (or alternatively, "hoarding function") will satisfy utility-maximization behavior of households over time since it maximizes the flow of utility from both the flow of commodities and the level of real balances. A detailed analysis of the size and stability of "absorption velocity" will be provided later in this chapter.

11. Lloyd Metzler, "Wealth, Saving and the Rate of Interest," *Journal of Political Economy,* 59 (April 1951), pp. 93-116.

12. For an economy as a whole the term "saving" is in this study meant to embrace *all* domestically produced output (consumption *and* investment goods) not bought by domestic residents.

13. For an analysis of the wealth/saving relationship in a growing economy see Miguel Sidrauski, "Rational Choice and Patterns of Growth in a Monetary Economy," *American Economic Review,* Papers and Proceedings, 57 (May 1967), pp. 543-544.

14. This automatic adjustment is not yet a feature of the absorption approach. In the absorption approach, policy measures such as "expenditure reducing" and "expenditure switching" may have to be introduced in order to bring about the desired change in the balance of payments. See, e.g., Harry G. Johnson, "The Balance of Payments," *Money, Trade and Economic Growth,* Harry G. Johnson (London: Allen & Unwin, 1962), pp. 15-27. An early approach which

incorporates an automatic adjustment of expenditure is presented by Prais, "Some Mathematical Notes on the Quantity Theory of Money in an Open Economy."

15. Archibald and Lipsey, "Monetary and Value Theory." This diagram has been called "one of the three basic diagrams of contemporary monetary theory." See Harry G. Johnson, "The Monetary Approach to the Balance of Payments," Discussion Paper, International Monetary Research Programme, London School of Economics, London, February 1975, p. 5.

16. The Archibald-Lipsey diagram has recently been applied to the analysis of economies as a whole by Johnson, "The Monetary Approach"; Peter D. Jonson and Henryk J. Kierzkowski, "The Balance of Payments: An Analytic Exercise," Discussion Paper, International Monetary Research Programme, London School of Economics, London, July 1974; Emil Maria Claassen, "Der monetäre Ansatz der Zahlungsbilanztheorie," *Weltwirtschaftliches Archiv,* 3, No. 1 (1975), pp. 1-23.

17. The monetary approach asserts that these variables do not change in the stationary state and grow at a stable rate in a growing world.

18. Most analyses of the role of money in an economy have been cast into the form of growth models. See, e.g., David Levhari and Don Patinkin, "The Role of Money in a Simple Growth Model," *American Economic Review,* 58 (September 1968), pp. 713-753; Harry G. Johnson, "Money in a Neo-Classical One-Sector Growth Model," *Essays in Monetary Economics,* 2nd ed., Harry G. Johnson (London: Allen & Unwin, 1969), chapter 4, pp. 143-178. For other types of exposition see Don Patinkin, *Money, Interest and Prices,* 2nd ed. (New York: Harper & Row, 1965), especially chapter 14, and Mundell, "Inflation, Hoarding and the Stationary State," especially pp. 50-54; Harry G. Johnson, "Inside Money, Outside Money, Income Wealth and Welfare in Monetary Theory," *Journal of Money, Credit and Banking,* 1, No. 1 (1969), pp. 30-45.

19. Levhari and Patinkin, "The Role of Money," p. 738.

20. The production function is "well behaved" in that the properties of (2.18) hold and additionally $k'(\bar{m}) \to \infty$ as $\bar{m} \to 0$; and $k'(\bar{m}) \to 0$ as $\bar{m} \to \infty$.

21. In a nonstationary economy equilibrium is expected to be brought about by the following adjustment processes. The substitution of capital for real balances subsequent to the rise in nominal balances raises the price of the given capital stock over the reproduction cost of capital. As a result, investment will be stimulated and the capital stock will rise. Assuming a diminishing marginal productivity of capital, both the *MPK*- and the $\bar{y}$-curves will shift downward, as shown by the broken lines in figure 2-1. The new equilibrium point will lie to the right of Q at Q$'$.

22. This utility function is employed by Miguel Sidrauski in his "Rational Choice and Patterns of Growth in a Monetary Economy," *American Economic Review* (Papers and Proceedings), 57 (May 1967), pp. 534-544.

23. See Karl Brunner and Allan H. Meltzer, "The Uses of Money: Money in

the Theory of an Exchange Economy," *American Economic Review,* 61 (December 1971), in particular, p. 797.

24. Ibid, p. 799.

25. Compare Basil K. Moore, *An Introduction to the Theory of Finance* (New York: The Free Press, 1968), especially pp. 16-17, and Brunner and Meltzer, "The Uses of Money," p. 800.

26. Compare Brunner and Meltzer, "The Uses of Money," p. 800.

27. Incidentally, this proposition is in line with the finding that "the secular rise in real income has been accompanied by a rise in real cash balances per unit of output—a decline in velocity." See Milton Friedman, "The Quantity Theory of Money: A Restatement," *The Optimum Quantity of Money and Other Essays* (London: Macmillan, 1969), p. 65.

28. Compare Mundell, "Inflation, Hoarding," pp. 50-54.

29. For this result compare Alvin L. Marty, "The Real Balance Effect: An Exercise in Capital Theory," *Canadian Journal of Economics and Political Science,* 30 (August 1964), pp. 360-367.

30. $\Sigma_{s=0}^{\infty} 1/(1+n)^s$ is the discount factor for real balances which emphasizes the "stock" characteristics of money, it is from now on denoted by *DF*. The nondiscounted indifference curve (given as a dashed curve U_e' in figure 2-4) has a slope equal to $-DF$ at the point of intersection with the vertical permanent-income line, point Q, and also at any point along the 0Q ray while the slope of the discounted equilibrium indifference curve is equal to -1.

31. Equation (2.30) follows from equation (2.28) $P = e \times P^*$ under the assumption that the foreign price level remains unchanged.

32. Given $m = M/P$ so that $\hat{m} = \hat{M} - \hat{P}$, equation (2.32) follows directly from equation (2.30) under the assumption of a constant money supply ($\hat{M} = 0$).

33. Unlike in the case in which two commodities enter the utility function, it cannot be assumed a priori that the U_{ij}'s are positive. In figure 2-2 above the assumption was made that U_{am} is equal to zero.

34. For an excellent and detailed description and explanation of the approach presented here and used throughout this section see Alpha C. Chiang, *Fundamental Methods of Mathematical Economics,* 2nd ed. (Tokyo, London: McGraw-Hill, 1974), pp. 373-402.

35. For simplicity it is assumed that $P^* = e = 1$ initially. Furthermore, $dM = dP^* = 0$.

36. Notice that dm/de in equation (2.34) is the expression for the endogenously generated change in the *demand* for real balances. The exogenously produced decline in the *supply* ($m = M/eP^*$) which results from the devaluation is equal to $-m$, as indicated in equation (2.36).

37. This result follows since the absolute value of the (negative) cofactor $|C_{32}|$ is smaller than the value of the Jacobian.

38. For simplicity it is assumed here that $\psi = 1$ and is constant over time. This latter assumption is, of course, unlikely to hold in reality. Empirical evi-

dence suggests rather that changes in the multiplier are quite substantial and often hard to predict in the short run, while in the long run a great degree of stability is observed. See, for example, Burger, "The Relationship between Monetary Base and Money."

39. The size of the absorption velocity λ is given by $tg\alpha$ in figure 2-4.

40. Since the marginal rate of time preference n is assumed to be constant over time it can be neglected in the following presentation of the dynamics of adjustment.

41. For an analysis of the path of adjustment of both the money supply and the balance of payments in a model which incorporates a delayed adjustment of the domestic price level rather than instantaneous adjustment, see Michael B. Connolly and Dean Taylor, "Devaluation, Traded Goods, and International Assets," *Recent Issues in International Monetary Economics,* ed. Emil M. Claassen and Pascal Salin (Amsterdam: North-Holland, 1976), pp. 53-64. A model which incorporates sluggish arbitrage will also be presented in a later part of this study.

42. Since a value of the absorption velocity λ greater than unity would imply that individuals intend to build up a level of real balances greater than the initial level, which is the desired level, it would be implausible to allow for a value of λ greater than unity.

43. Compare Swoboda, "Monetary Approaches."

44. Compare ibid.

45. For an analysis of "real" and "monetary" changes in the large country case see Johnson, "The Monetary Approach." This article shows that in a large-country setting and given the world quantity of money it is the world price level and the distribution of money among countries which adjust to an exogenous disturbance.

46. Notice that in equilibrium $U_m = U_b$, hence the marginal utility of total wealth will adopt the same value as the marginal utility of its components.

47. Compare the remarks on p. 28.

48. Equations (2.47) to (2.49) hold since dG/de is equal to $-(b + m)$. This result is obtained by substituting equation (2.28) into equation (2.44), assuming for simplicity that $P^* = e = 1$ initially, and differentiating (2.44) with respect to e.

49. It can be demonstrated by an easy transformation of the excess demand equations that the sum of the excess demands for goods, bonds, and money is zero. Recall that the sum of the excess demands for a, b, and m is

$$(b + m)\,|C_{41}|/|J| + [(b + m)\,|C_{42}|/|J| + b] + [(b + m)\,|C_{43}|/|J| + m]\,.$$

Adding the separate components b and m and multiplying the transformed sum of the excess demands by $|J|/(b + m)$ yields the condition for a zero value of the sum of the excess demands:

$$|C_{41}| + |C_{42}| + |C_{43}| + |J| = 0$$

Matrix algebra holds that for any matrix M the sum of the products of the row elements of any row times the corresponding cofactors is equal to the value of the matrix, e.g.,

$$M = a_{41}\ |C_{41}| + a_{42}\ |C_{42}| + a_{43}\ |C_{43}| + a_{44}\ |C_{44}|$$

Since, in the above example, $a_{41} = a_{42} = a_{43} = -1$ and $a_{44} = 0$, the sum of the first-period excess demands generated by the devaluation is, indeed, zero.

50. A more detailed examination of the adjustment processes in the financial markets with a particular emphasis on the path of adjustment of the domestic interest rate is provided in chapter 3.

51. Notice that by the Stolper-Samuelson theorem the relative price of capital is inversely related to the yield on real capital, $r = P/Pk$, so that the real value of bonds in terms of consumption is equal to $b = K/r$ [compare equation (2.42)].

52. It has been suggested in an earlier section of chapter 2 that absorption velocity is inversely related to the marginal rate of time preference. The results presented here can, therefore, also be interpreted in terms of absorption velocity.

53. Claassen assumes a constant expansion path for the portfolio equilibrium in his diagrammatic presentation. He thus neglects entirely the financing requirements related to the given level of desired absorption. Compare Claassen, "Der monetäre Ansatz," p. 17.

54. The decline in domestically owned foreign bonds involves a decline in net interest receipts from abroad. This reduces real disposable income (given by y_0 in figure 2-8). In order not to overcharge the diagrammatic presentation this decline in real income is not depicted in the diagram and is not taken into account in the verbal explanation of the adjustment process.

55. This assumes, of course, that real balances required to finance imports are not directly offset by real balances obtained for exports. Allowing for this assumption, the amount of bond sales required to obtain real balances for the financing of a level of absorption equal to a_1 would be only BC - CE where CE is the trade-account surplus of the first period. The above approach has been chosen for its greater clarity of presentation. The results with respect to the development of subbalances of the balance of payments are changed only in their magnitude, not in their direction.

56. This assumes that the home country is an international lender. If the home country is a net international debtor, the final equilibrium will be marked by a trade-account surplus and a matching service-account deficit. Notice that the adjustment in the subaccounts as described above holds strictly only in the case of an instantaneous adjustment of the domestic price level; it will be different in the case of a gradual rise in domestic prices.

57. This appears to be suggested by James Tobin in his "A General Equilibrium Approach to Monetary Theory," *Journal of Money, Credit and Banking,* 1, No. 1 (1969), p. 16.

Chapter 3
Devaluation and Portfolio Adjustment

1. For an excellent general portfolio-equilibrium model which concentrates on the stock adjustment processes between four imperfectly substitutable assets, two of which are nontraded, see William H. Branson, "Portfolio Equilibrium and Monetary Policy with Foreign and Non-traded Assets," *Recent Issues in International Monetary Economics,* ed. Emil M. Claassen and Pascal Salin (Amsterdam: North-Holland, 1976), pp. 241–250. A model which investigates both stock and flow aspects of portfolio balance behavior is presented by the same author in his "Stocks and Flows in International Monetary Analysis," *Aspects of Stabilization Policies,* ed. Albert Ando, Richard Herring, and Richard Marston, Federal Reserve Bank of Boston Conference Series No. 12 (Boston, 1974), pp. 27–50. In this chapter the basic structure of the latter model is adopted for the analysis of portfolio balance behavior in response to a devaluation.

2. Money is assumed to bear a zero rate of interest.

3. In the first section of the analysis, the assumption is made that money is a producer's good so that the demand for it is determined by income (= value of output). Later, the implications of money as a consumer's good will be considered; money demand will then be a function of absorption rather than income. The incorporation of income as an explanatory variable in asset-demand functions stresses the importance of the transactions motive for the demand for real balances. In a recent empirical study on the United States Meyer and Neri conclude that the transactions motive overrides the asset motive for holding money. They state that "finance requirements and not assets explain money demand" (p. 619). See A. Meyer and John A. Neri, "A Keynes-Friedman Money Demand Function," *American Economic Review,* 65 (September 1975), pp. 610–623.

4. Since by assumption full-employment output is constant, any movement along the abscissa implies a change of the price level. A movement along the abscissa therefore measures a change in nominal income rather than real income.

5. Notice that if the domestic bond were a tradable rather than a nontradable asset, the slope of the BB curve would be flatter than it is in the nontradable case. This follows from the fact that the aggregate demand function for B would include foreign demand, F^{BF} so that $B = F^{B}(r, r^*, Y)\,W + F^{BF}(r, r^*)\,W^*$. The slope of the BB curve is then given by the equation, $dr/dy|_{BB} = -F_Y^B/(F_r^B + F_r^{BF})$, which proves the above proposition. The assumption that all

domestic bonds are nontraded is a simplification which puts into sharp relief the adjustment processes between imperfectly substitutable assets. Nontraded bonds (mortgages, equities of small companies with local significance, etc.) may play a significant role in any economy, and, thus, the above simplification does not appear to be unduly unrealistic. For a discussion of the importance of nontraded assets in national economies, see Tibor Scitovski, *Money and the Balance of Payments* (London: Allen & Unwin, 1969). For a model with two traded but imperfectly substitutable assets in a large-country setting, see Lance Girton and Dale W. Henderson, "Critical Determinants of the Effectiveness of Monetary Policy in the Open Economy," mimeographed, Board of Governors, Federal Reserve System, September 1974.

6. Compare Branson, "Stocks and Flows," p. 31.

7. The result follows from differentiation of equation (3.3) with respect to the exchange rate. Notice that for a constant real income y the change in nominal income $Y = y \times P$ is equal to ydP/de. Given perfect and instantaneous goods arbitrage, dP/de equals unity.

8. Recall that thus far money is considered a pure producer's good, hence the value of output Y enters the demand function instead of nominal absorption A.

9. If the country is a net debtor, devaluation raises the value of domestic debt to foreigners measured in domestic currency and, thus, lowers nominal wealth of the economy. Notice that the home country can become a net debtor only if, in contrast to the assumption made in this chapter, domestic assets become internationally tradable.

10. Notice that, ceteris paribus, and given a fixed level of output, any change in nominal income is the reflection of a change in the exchange rate and, thus, the domestic price level. Equally, a change in nominal wealth–given M, B and B^*, as must be assumed to describe the impact effect of a devaluation–is the expression of a change in the exchange rate.

11. A similar diagrammatic technique has been espoused by Russel S. Boyer in his "Devaluation and Portfolio Balance," Discussion Paper, International Monetary Research Programme, London School of Economics and Political Science, March 1975. Boyer concentrates on the first-period instantaneous equilibrium in the market for domestic bonds and domestic nontraded goods.

12. Notice that the sequence of steps toward portfolio equilibrium described here is somewhat arbitrary. Generally it is assumed in economic models that a simultaneous adjustment in the components of the portfolio and an immediate achievement of portfolio equilibrium takes place if full information can be assumed and transactions costs are absent. The approach chosen here abandons this assumption and thereby sheds some more light on the decision-making processes involved in portfolio management.

13. The above presentation highlights the influence of wealth and portfolio adjustment effects on domestic price behavior and abstracts at this stage from

the direct price or arbitrage effect more commonly used in devaluation analysis. Given the fact that adjustments in the goods markets are generally slower than those in asset markets and therefore goods arbitrage may be sluggish, the wealth and portfolio adjustment effect may be the more relevant effects for the first period after a change in the exchange rate.

14. Recall that the net effect on real wealth must be negative regardless of whether the home country is a net creditor or debtor; the only exception is the unlikely case that all wealth consists of foreign bonds, in which case real wealth remains unchanged. Compare equation (2.54).

15. In terms of the diagram, $F_Y^B = 0$ means a horizontal BB curve.

16. This follows from $F_Y^{B*} - F_Y^B (F_r^{B*}/F_r^B) < F_Y^{B*}$ where the right-hand term expresses the case of $F_Y^B = 0$ in equation (3.13).

17. A number of simplifications are included in this result. Both the initial values of e and P are set equal to unity. B^* is then equal to b^* and w equal to W. Notice that $(w - \bar{w})$ is equal to zero in equilibrium but equal to dw/de, as a result of the impact effect of a change in the exchange rate and before any variation in the interest rate has taken place.

18. The inverse relation between absorption and the interest rate which accounts for the negative slope of the AA lines is derived from a differentiation of (3.17) with respect to r. For an interpretation of the behavioral factors which determine the slope of the AA lines, see the text.

19. Notice that it is theoretically conceivable that the interest rate declines. This is the case if absorption velocity is very high so that the AA_1 curve intersects the BB_1 curve to the left of point S in figure 3-5. The presentation of the path of adjustment in chapter 2 suggests, however, that this is an unlikely case in reality.

20. This trade-account surplus in nominal terms corresponds to the balance-of-payments surplus in real terms denoted by $y_0 - a_1'$ in figure 2-6. Both figures include the effects of a variation in the domestic interest rate on absorption velocity and on the income velocity of circulation of money.

Chapter 4
Traded and Nontraded Goods in Devaluation Analysis

1. The distinction between traded and nontraded goods and an evaluation of the importance of this distinction for the international adjustment process of dependent economies was introduced into economic thinking in the late 1950s and early 1960s by Salter and Swan. See W.E. Salter, "Internal and External Balance: The Role of Price and Expenditure Effects," *Economic Record,* 35 (August 1959), pp. 226-238; T.W. Swan, "Economic Control in a Dependent Economy," *Economic Record,* 36 (August 1959), pp. 51-66; T.W. Swan, "Longer Run Problems of the Balance of Payments," *The Australian Economy:*

A Volume of Readings, ed. H.W. Arndt and M.W. Corden (Melbourne: F.W. Cheshire, 1963). More recent studies of the importance of nontraded goods for international adjustment include Robert A. Mundell, *Monetary Theory: Inflation, Interest and Growth in the World Economy* (Pacific Palisades, Calif.: Goodyear, 1971); Richard E. Caves and Ronald W. Jones, *World Trade and Payments* (Boston: Little, Brown, 1973), supplement to chapter 19, pp. 409–413; Rüdiger Dornbusch, "Real and Monetary Aspects of the Effects of Exchange Rate Changes," *National Monetary Policies and the International Financial System,* ed. Robert Z. Aliber (Chicago: University of Chicago Press, 1974), pp. 64–81; Rüdiger Dornbusch, "Alternative Price Stabilization Rules and the Effects of Exchange Rate Changes," Discussion Paper, revised version, October 1974; Peter D. Jonson and Henryk J. Kierzkowski, "The Balance of Payments: An Analytical Exercise," Discussion Paper, International Monetary Research Programme, London School of Economics and Political Science, July 1974; Ronald W. Jones and W. Max Corden, "Devaluation, Price Rigidities, and the Trade Balance for a Small Country," Discussion Paper, International Monetary Research Programme, London School of Economics and Political Science, August 1974. A rather complete algebraic treatment of the importance of nontraded goods in a model with independent import- and export-goods price determination is provided by J.F. Pearce, "The Problem of the Balance of Payments." *International Economic Review,* 2 (January 1961), pp. 1–28. The presentation in this chapter draws on the above research and applies it to the analysis of exchange-rate changes.

2. In a recent empirical study of the United Kingdom, Cross and Laidler distinguish four groups of commodities and services which fall into the category of nontraded goods: housing, services, gas and electricity, and transport services. The weight of nontradables in total expenditure is estimated to be equal to 21 percent in 1968. See Rodney Cross and David Laidler, "Inflation, Excess Demand and Expectations in Fixed Exchange Rate Open Economies: Some Preliminary Empirical Results," *Inflation in the World Economy,* ed. Michael Parkin and George Zis (Manchester: Manchester University Press, 1976), pp. 221–254.

3. In this section of the analysis, use is made of the most simple absorption function. It contains real balances as the only form of wealth and thus neglects portfolio adjustment processes and the effects of variations of interest rates. The results of a model which uses the more comprehensive absorption function developed in previous chapters are presented in a later part of this chapter.

4. In this simple version of the model, the home country is assumed to hold zero foreign assets; it is neither a foreign lender nor a foreign debtor. Hence, there are no interest flows between countries which could lead to a deviation between the value of domestic output and domestic income.

5. Compare Dornbusch, "Real and Monetary Aspects," p. 3.

6. Real income appears to fall in terms of traded goods and to rise in terms of nontraded goods. However, given full-employment output at both point

Q and also at point D, there appears to be no reason to assume that real income has changed at all. By choosing a price index with variable weights, it can be shown that real income measures in terms of money prices of commodities remains indeed constant along the transformation curve. Compare Boyer, "Commodity Markets," footnote 5, p. 24.

7. In the absence of perfect arbitrage in traded goods, the immediate rise in the price level is given by $dP = \beta de$, where β is the share of imports in total expenditure.

8. Equation (4.17) follows from a differentiation of equation (4.10) after the substitution of (4.1) and (4.15) into (4.10). Notice that, by assumption, $P = P^N = e = 1$ initially.

9. Dornbusch demonstrates that a rise in the price of home goods can be prevented and the consumption point G be reached if appropriate fiscal and/or monetary policy measures are taken which cut back private demand to that level. Both a rise in taxes and a decline in the money supply will lead to a downward shift of the disposable-income line" CA until it intersects the expenditure-consumption line at point G. As can be read from figure 4-3, such a policy would generally enhance the effect of a devaluation on the trade balance: the trade surplus in this case (GD) is visibly larger than the trade surplus in the case of an upward adjustment in the price of home goods in response to an excess demand in this market (G′D′). For an appraisal of Dornbusch's analysis see his paper: "Alternative Price Stabilization Rules."

10. Compare Jonson and Kierzkowski: "The Balance of Payments," p. 20.

11. For an analysis of the changes involved when turning to a more comprehensive wealth concept, see chapters 2 and 3.

12. For the derivation of (4.24), compare equation (4.17) and footnote 2, chapter 4. Notice also that $b^*/w = F^{B^*}$. For a detailed description of the substitution and the real balance effect, compare pages 83-85.

13. Recall that, on the other hand, the effect of a rise in the interest rate on the income velocity of circulation tends to reduce the speed of adjustment. Compare chapters 2 and 3.

Chapter 5
The Importance of Money Illusion for the Adjustment Process

1. This behavior is generally referred to as "cost plus pricing."

2. For simplicity of exposition it is assumed here that nontraded goods are produced at constant returns to scale. Furthermore, no allowance is made for an increased income velocity of circulation which would temporarily shift the CD line away from the origin.

3. W. Max Corden, *Monetary Integration,* Essays in International Finance, No. 93, International Finance Section, Princeton University, Princeton, N.J.,

1972, p. 12. See also Robert A. Mundell, "A Theory of Optimum Currency Areas," *American Economic Review,* 51 (November 1961), pp. 657-665; Ronald J. McKinnon, "Optimum Currency Areas," *American Economic Review,* 53 (September 1963), pp. 717-724; Robert A. Mundell, "Discussion," *Canadian United States Financial Relationships,* Federal Reserve Bank of Boston Conference Series No. 6 (Boston: Federal Reserve Bank of Boston, 1971), pp. 47-49.

4. Compare Corden, *Monetary Integration,* p. 12. Compare also the situation described in chapter 4.

5. The view that money illusion may be detrimental to the process of balance-of-payments adjustment has recently been advanced by J.C. Murphy and S.K. Das, "Money Illusion and Balance-of-Payments Adjustment," *Journal of Political Economy,* 84, No. 1 (1976), pp. 73-82.

6. The decline in real wealth is also immediately realized as a result of the decline in the nominal value of net foreign assets (eB^*) by $-edB^*$. Net foreign assets decline because the home country borrows from abroad (or sells foreign bonds, as the case may be).

7. The importance of the organization of the labor market and the strength and motivation of trade unions for the adjustment process has also been realized by Murphy and Das, "Money Illusion."

8. This assumes that domestic residents do not raise their wage demands in response to the deterioration of their real income and wealth position.

9. Real incomes of employed workers will remain stable because by assumption, the rise in the nominal wage rate equals the rise in the price level. However, aggregate real income declines because of unemployment; the ensuing decline in demand furthers the improvement in the trade balance. It has to be noticed, however, that in modern societies with well-established unemployment insurance schemes, there will be a certain automatism which prevents to some extent a favorable adjustment in the trade balance after a devaluation. Unemployment insurance serves as an automatic stabilizer for aggregate demand. When unemployment arises, unemployment compensation is paid. The financing of the compensation may partly or entirely take the form of money creation, depending on the financing arrangements for the insurance scheme. As a result, aggregate demand remains at a rather high level despite the fact that a section of the labor force is unemployed. This tends to undercut the positive effects of a devaluation.

10. If, in a situation of chronic overspending of a country, devaluation is used as a means of reducing domestic real demand and thereby improving the balance of payments, it appears to be unlikely that residents will be prepared to accept a decline in their real incomes where they were not before. In this situation, a devaluation may not cure the situation if the authorities maintain a full employment policy. If, on the other hand, the authorities decide against financing higher wage demands resulting from a devaluation, a devaluation may be successful, as is demonstrated above. However, in this case it would not require

a devaluation to cure the situation. The country could simply adopt a restrictive monetary policy in the first place. As to the relative merits of a restrictive monetary policy versus a devaluation see the conclusions in chapter 7.

Chapter 6
Price Expectations and the Adjustment Process

1. The basic reasoning for this type of behavior is similar to the one expounded by Milton Friedman in his permanent income hypothesis of consumption: it is long-term expected income (wealth) which determines spending behavior; short-term fluctuations leave spending largely unaffected. See Milton Friedman, *A Theory of the Consumption Function,* National Bureau of Economic Research, vol. 63, General Series (Princeton, N.J.: Princeton University Press, 1957). There is, however, one reason that the community should reduce spending even if it expects prices to rise only temporarily. As prices rise, the money supply is unfit to finance real income and expenditure in the present period. In the absence of an expansionary monetary policy, capital imports will have to meet the excess demand for money. The home country becomes a net foreign debtor (or reduces its net foreign asset position). The related interest payments to abroad (reduced receipts from abroad) lower real income throughout the time span during which the domestic price level lies above the "equilibrium" price level and thus requires borrowing from abroad. Hence, there is a rationale—though perhaps of little importance—for reducing present expenditure even if the decline in wealth due to the rise in prices is not expected to last.

2. An early key note on the forms of and reasons for price expectations is contained in John R. Hicks, *Value and Capital* (London: Oxford University Press, 1939), especially pp. 204-205. For an excellent, more recent evaluation of price expectations, see John H. Power, "Price Expectations, Money Illusion, and the Real Balance Effect," *Journal of Political Economy,* 67 (1959), pp. 131-143.

3. Compare Power: "Price Expectations," pp. 136-138.

4. This effect on spending decisions has been dubbed the "Wicksell effect" by James Tobin. Tobin views the Wicksell effect as working in the opposite direction to the Pigou effect which is the wealth effect described above. Compare James Tobin, "Money and Economic Growth," *Econometrica,* 33 no. 4 (October 1965) pp. 671-684. Power calls the former effect the "intertemporal substitution effect." Compare Power, "Price Expectations," p. 134.

5. Compare Miguel Sidrauski, "Inflation and Economic Growth," *Journal of Political Economy,* 75 (December 1967), pp. 804-805.

6. See the important study by Philip Cagan on hyperinflations. Philip Cagan, "The Monetary Dynamics of Hyperinflations," *Studies in the Quantity Theory of Money,* ed. Milton Friedman (Chicago: University of Chicago Press, 1956), pp. 25-117.

7. Compare Sidrauski, "Inflation and Economic Growth," p. 805.

8. In two recent studies Juster and Wachtel investigate the behavior of consumers in an inflationary environment. In their studies, they distinguish between anticipated and unanticipated inflation. The econometric testing procedure applies quarterly data on the United States from 1954, second quarter, through 1971, second quarter. The studies prove that "unanticipated inflation does cause the household to reallocate income toward saving and away from spending." On the other hand, "fully anticipated inflation raises consumption expenditure on non-durables and services at the expense of both saving and expenditure on durables." See F. Thomas Juster and Paul Wachtel: "Inflation and the Consumer," *Brookings Papers on Economic Activity,* 1972, no. 1, (Washington, D.C.: Brookings Institution, 1972), pp. 71-114, here pp. 101-102. For additional information on the nexus between anticipated inflation and spending behavior see also F. Thomas Juster and Paul Wachtel: "A Note on Inflation and the Saving Rate," *Brookings Papers on Economic Activity,* 1972, no. 3 (Washington, D.C.: Brookings Institution, 1972), pp. 765-778. On the basis of their empirical evidence, these two studies appear to support the above view that anticipated inflation leads to a hastening of purchases.

9. For simplicity the absorption function employs money as the only form of wealth. The results obtained below do not change in quality if a more comprehensive concept of wealth is applied.

10. P_{EL} will also remain constant if past price experience has not indicated any clearly discernible trend in prices. Economic agents will then take the pre-devaluation price level as a best guess for the future one.

11. Equation (6.2) expresses a form of the "extrapolative expectations hypothesis." The results obtained below would be similar if one would assume the existence of "adaptive expectations" in which case $P^e - P^e_{-1} = \pi (P - P^e_{-1})$ or $P^e = \pi P + (1 - \pi) P^e_{-1}$ where P^e is the price expected in the current period for the next period.

12. In the small-country case only the prices of nontraded goods can temporarily exceed their long-run equilibrium values. The small-country assumption implies that traded goods prices are at all times determined by the prices prevailing in the rest of the world. These are by assumption invariable. If the home country is a large country, overshooting is also possible in traded goods prices.

13. For the method employed and the basic equations used compare chapter 2. Recall again that in this study $\bar{e}$ is used to express the natural exponential function whereas e is the exchange rate.

14. Notice that the acceptance by the public of a permanent increase in the velocity of circulation would imply a reduction in the desired level of real balances, $L/P = ky = (1/v)y$, where v is the income velocity of circulation of money. A permanent rise of v is, thus, not compatible with the assumption of a stable long-run money-demand function throughout this study.

15. In the models presented so far a strengthening of the contingency-reserve motive is reflected in an increased level of desired real wealth.

16. Figure 6-1 reveals that, because of the interaction of the wealth and

intertemporal distribution effect, and under the assumptions made about long-run and short-run price expectations, there exists the possibility that the trade balance might display a J-curve effect.

17. Compare Connolly and Taylor, "Devaluation," p. 55.

Chapter 7
Conclusions and Policy Implications

1. The devaluation of the pound sterling by 8.6 percent on December 21, 1971, was preceded by a growth in the British money supply by 15.3 percent in 1971 and followed by a growth of the money supply by 13.9 percent in 1972. In 1972, exports rose by 6.2 percent, imports by 13.4 percent. This indicates the complete failure of the authorities' exchange-rate and monetary policy intended to cure the British balance-of-payments difficulties.

2. After the suspension of the pound sterling on September 21, 1931, the British currency was on the average effectively devalued by about 30 percent. The money supply rose by about 1.0 percent in 1931, by 1.8 percent in 1932, and by 7.9 percent in 1933. The deficit in the trade balance was reduced by almost 45 percent in 1932 and by more than 53 percent in 1933 as compared with the deficit in 1931. This proves the relative success of the devaluation.

3. Johnson, "The Monetary Approach to the Balance of Payments," pp. 7-8. Notice that the capital gain on the value of the existing stock of foreign reserves which occurs in the case of a devaluation is neglected in the following discussion.

4. For this point compare Johnson, "The Monetary Approach to the Balance of Payments," (1975), pp. 10-11.

5. For an account of the effects of exchange-rate rigidity in a growing world, see Robert M. Dunn, Jr., *Exchange-Rate Rigidity, Investment Distortions and the Failure of Bretton Woods,* Essays in International Finance, No. 97 (Princeton, N.J.: Princeton University Press, 1973).

6. In a growing world, this does not necessarily have to be a decline, but a less than proportionate increase in their real incomes compared with the growth of output.

Bibliography

Alexander, Sidney S., "Effects of a Devaluation on a Trade Balance," *Staff Papers,* 2, no. 2 (Washington, D.C.: International Monetary Fund, April 1952), pp. 263-278.

Amano, A., "Nontraded Goods and Effects of Devaluation," *Economic Studies Quarterly,* 23, no. 2 (August 1972), pp. 1-19.

Archibald, G.C., and Lipsey, R.G., "Monetary and Value Theory: A Critique of Lange and Patinkin," *Review of Economic Studies,* 26 (October 1958), pp. 1-22.

Balassa, Bela, "The Purchasing Power Parity Theorem: A Reappraisal," *Journal of Political Economy,* 72 (1964), pp. 584-596.

Batra, Raveendra N., "Nontraded Goods, Factor Market Distortions, and Gains from Trade," *American Economic Review,* 63, no. 4 (1973), pp. 706-713.

Bender, Dieter, *Abwertung und Gesamtwirtschaftliches Gleichgewicht,* Volkswirtschaftliche Schriften, Heft 190 (Berlin: Duncker & Humblot, 1972).

Berglas, Eitan, "Devaluation, Monetary Policy, and Border Tax Adjustments," *Canadian Journal of Economics,* 71, no. 1 (February 1974), pp. 1-11.

Boyer, Russell S., "Commodity Markets and Bond Markets in a Small Fixed Exchange-Rate Economy," Discussion Paper, International Monetary Research Programme, London School of Economics and Political Science (April 1974).

Boyer, Russell S., "Devaluation and Portfolio Balance," Discussion Paper, International Monetary Research Programme, London School of Economics and Political Science (March 1975).

Boyer, Russell S., "Fixed Rates, Flexible Rates, and the International Transmission of Inflation," Discussion Paper, International Monetary Research Programme, London School of Economics and Political Science (April 1975).

Branson, William, *Financial Capital Movements in the U.S. Balance of Payments* (Amsterdam: North-Holland, 1968).

Branson, William, "Portfolio Equilibrium and Monetary Policy with Foreign and Non-Traded Assets," Recent Issues in International Monetary Economics, ed. Emil M. Claassen and Pascal Salin, (Amsterdam: North-Holland, 1976), pp. 241-250.

Branson, William, "Stocks and Flows in International Monetary Analysis," *International Aspects of Stabilisation Policies,* ed. Albert Ando, Richard Herring, and Richard Marston (Boston: Federal Reserve Bank of Boston Conference Series no. 12 (June 1974), pp. 27-50.

Branson, William, "Monetarist and Keynesian Models of the Transmission of Inflation," *American Economic Review* (Papers and Proceedings) 63 (May 1975), pp. 115-119.

Brunner, Karl, "Money Supply Process and Monetary Policy in an Open Economy," *International Trade and Money,* ed. Michael Connolly and Alexander K. Swoboda (London: Allen & Unwin, 1973), pp. 127-166.

Brunner, Karl, and Meltzer, Allan H., "The Uses of Money: Money in the Theory of an Exchange Economy," *American Economic Review,* 61 (December 1971), pp. 784-805.

Burger, Albert, *The Money Supply Process* (Belmont, Calif.: Wadsworth, 1971).

Burger, Albert, "The Relationship between Monetary Base and Money: How Close?" *Federal Reserve Bank of St. Louis Review* (October 1975), pp. 3-8.

Cagan, Philip, "The Monetary Dynamics of Hyperinflation," *Studies in the Quantity Theory of Money,* ed. Milton Friedman (Chicago: University of Chicago Press, 1956), pp. 25-117.

Caves, Richard E., and Jones, Ronald W., *World Trade and Payments: An Introduction* (Boston: Little, Brown, 1973).

Chiang, Alpha C., *Fundamental Methods of Mathematical Economics,* 2nd ed. (Tokyo, London: McGraw-Hill, 1974).

Claassen, Emil-Maria, "Der monetäre Ansatz der Zahlungsbilanztheorie," *Weltwirtschaftliches Archiv,* 3, no. 1 (1975), pp. 1-23.

Collery, Arnold P., *International Adjustment, Open Economies, and the Quantity Theory of Money,* Princeton Studies in International Finance, no. 28 (Princeton: International Finance Section, Department of Economics, Princeton University, 1971).

Connolly, Michael, and Taylor, Dean, "Devaluation, Traded Goods, and International Assets," *Recent Issues in International Economics,* ed. Emil M. Claassen and Pascal Salin (Amsterdam: North-Holland, 1976), pp. 53-63.

Cooper, Richard N., "Monetary Theory and Policy in an Open Economy," *The Scandinavian Journal of Economics,* 78, no. 2 (1976), pp. 146-163.

Corden, W. Max, *Monetary Integration,* Essays in International Finance, no. 93 (Princeton: International Finance Section, Department of Economics, Princeton University, 1972).

Cross, Rodney, and Laidler, David, "Inflation, Excess Demand and Expectations in Fixed Exchange Rate Open Economies: Some Preliminary Empirical Results," *Inflation in the World Economy,* ed. Michael Parkin and George Zis (Manchester: Manchester University Press, 1976), pp. 221-254.

Dornbusch, Rüdiger, "Devaluation, Money, and Nontraded Goods," *American Economic Review,* 63 (1973), pp. 871-880.

Dornbusch, Rüdiger, "Currency Depreciation, Hoarding, and Relative Prices," *Journal of Political Economy,* 81 (July/August 1973), pp. 893-915.

Dornbusch, Rüdiger, "Capital Mobility, Flexible Exchange Rates, and Macroeconomic Equilibrium," *Recent Issues in International Monetary Economics,* ed. Emil M. Claassen and Pascal Salin (Amsterdam: North-Holland, 1976), pp. 261-278.

Dornbusch, Rüdiger, "Capital Mobility and Portfolio Balance," Discussion Paper, International Monetary Research Programme, London School of Economics and Political Science, revised version (June 1974).

Dornbusch, Rüdiger, "Alternative Price Stabilisation Rules and the Effects of Exchange Rate Changes," revised version of a paper presented at a Money Study Group Meeting in honor of James E. Meade at Merton College (Oxford University, September 25-27, 1974).

Dornbusch, Rüdiger, "Real and Monetary Aspects of the Effects of Exchange Rate Changes," *National Monetary Policies and the International Financial System,* ed. Robert Z. Aliber (Chicago: University of Chicago Press, 1974), pp. 64-81.

Dornbusch, Rüdiger, "Flexible Exchange Rates and Capital Mobility: Some Notes on the Argy-Porter Model," Discussion Paper, University of Chicago (1975).

Dornbusch, Rüdiger, "A Portfolio Balance Model of the Open Economy," *Journal of Monetary Economics,* 1, no. 1 (1975), pp. 3-20.

Dornbusch, Rüdiger, "The Theory of Flexible Exchange Rate Regimes and Macroeconomic Policy," *The Scandinavian Journal of Economics,* 78, no. 2 (1976), pp. 255-275.

Dornbusch, Rüdiger, and Mussa, Michael, "Consumption, Real Balances and the Hoarding Function," *International Economic Review,* 16 (1975), pp. 415-421.

Dunn, Robert M., Jr., *Exchange Rate Rigidity, Investment Distortions and the Failure of Bretton Woods,* Essays in International Finance, no. 97, (Princeton, International Finance Section, Department of Economics, Princeton University, 1973).

Ethier, Wilfred, "Nontraded Goods in the Heckscher-Ohlin Model," *International Economic Review,* 13, no. 1 (1972), pp. 132-147.

Federal Reserve Bank of Boston, *Canadian-United States Financial Relationships, Proceedings of a Conference,* Federal Reserve Bank of Boston Conferences, series no. 6 (Boston, 1971).

Feber, Robert, "Consumer Economics: A Survey," *Journal of Economic Literature,* 11, no. 4 (1973), pp. 1303-1342.

Floyd, John E., "Monetary and Fiscal Policy in a World of Capital Mobility," *Review of Economic Studies,* 36 (1959), pp. 503-517.

Frenkel, Jacob, "Adjustment Mechanisms and the Monetary Approach to the Balance of Payments: A Doctrinal Perspective," *Recent Issues in International Monetary Economics,* ed. Emil M. Claassen and Pascal Salin (Amsterdam: North-Holland, 1976), pp. 29-48.

Frenkel, Jacob, and Johnson, Harry G. (eds.), *The Monetary Approach to the Balance of Payments* (London: Allen & Unwin, 1976).

Frenkel, Jacob and Rodriguez, Carlos A., "Portfolio Equilibrium and the Balance of Payments: A Monetary Approach," *American Economic Review,* 65 (September 1975), pp. 674-688.

Friedman, Milton, "The Quantity Theory of Money: A Restatement," *Studies in the Quantity Theory of Money,* ed. Milton Friedman (Chicago: University of Chicago Press, 1956), pp. 3-21.

Friedman, Milton, *A Theory of the Consumption Function,* NBER, no. 63, general series (Princeton, N.J.: Princeton University Press, 1957).

Friedman, Milton, *The Optimum Quantity of Money and Other Essays* (London: Macmillan, 1969).

Friedman, Milton, "A Theoretical Framework for Monetary Analysis," *Journal of Political Economy,* 78 (1970), pp. 193-238.

Genberg, Hans, and Kierzkowski, Henryk, "Short Run, Long Run and Dynamics of Adjustment under Flexible Exchange Rates," Research Paper, National Economic Policy and the International Monetary System, The Graduate Institute of International Studies, Geneva (June 1975).

Girton, Lance, and Henderson, Dale W., "Critical Determinants of the Effectiveness of Monetary Policy in an Open Economy," Discussion Paper, Board of Governors, Federal Reserve System (September 3, 1974).

Harberger, Arnold C., "Currency Depreciation, Income and the Balance of Trade," *Journal of Political Economy,* 58 (February 1950), pp. 47-60.

Henderson, Dale W., "Monetary, Fiscal, and Exchange Rate Policy in a Two Country, Short Run, Macroeconomic Model," Discussion Paper, revised draft, Board of Governors, Federal Reserve System (December 1974).

Hicks, John R., *Value and Capital* (London: Oxford University Press, 1939).

Hume, David, "Of the Balance of Trade," Excerpts from D. Hume (1952), *Essays, Moral, Political and Literary* (London: 1898), pp. 330-341 and 343-345, reprinted in *International Finance, Selected Readings,* ed. R.N. Cooper (Harmondsworth: Penguin Books, 1969), pp. 25-37.

International Monetary Fund, *The Monetary Approach to the Balance of Payments* (Washington, D.C.: International Monetary Fund, 1977).

Jacob, Klaus Dieter, *Wechselkurs und Leistungsbilanz* (Berlin: De Gruyter, 1972).

Johnson, Harry G., "Towards a General Theory of the Balance of Payments," *International Trade and Economic Growth,* Harry G. Johnson (London: Allen & Unwin, 1958), pp. 153-168.

Johnson, Harry G., "The Balance of Payments," *Money, Trade and Economic Growth,* Harry G. Johnson (London: Allen & Unwin, 1962), pp. 15-27.

Johnson, Harry G., "Money in a Neo-Classical One-Sector Growth Model," *Essays in Monetary Economics,* Harry G. Johnson (London: Allen & Unwin, 1969), pp. 143-178.

Johnson, Harry G., "Inside Money, Outside Money, Income, Wealth and Welfare in Monetary Theory," *Journal of Money, Credit, and Banking,* 1, no. 1 (1969), pp. 30-45.

Johnson, Harry G., "The Monetary Approach to Balance of Payments Theory," *International Trade and Money,* ed. Michael B. Connolly and Alexander K. Swoboda (London: Allen & Unwin, 1973), pp. 206-224.

Johnson, Harry G., "The Monetary Approach to the Balance of Payments," Discussion Paper, International Monetary Research Programme, London School of Economics and Political Science (February 1975).

Johnson, Harry G., "Balance of Payments Adjustment with Bonds and Goods: A Geometrical Approach," Discussion Paper, International Monetary Research

Programme, London School of Economics and Political Science (February 1975).

Johnson, Harry G., "Elasticity, Absorption, Keynesian Multiplier, Keynesian Policy, and Monetary Approaches to Devaluation Theory: A Simple Geometric Exposition," *American Economic Review,* 66 (June 1976), pp. 448-452.

Jones, Ronald W., and Corden, W. Max, "Devaluation, Price Rigidities and the Trade Balance for a Small Country," Discussion Paper, International Monetary Research Programme, London School of Economics and Political Science (August 1974).

Jonson, Peter D., and Kierzkowski, Henryk I., "The Balance of Payments: An Analytical Exercise," Discussion Paper, International Monetary Research Programme, London School of Economics and Political Science (July 1974).

Juster, F. Thomas, and Wachtel, Paul, "Inflation and the Consumer," in *Brookings Papers on Economic Activity,* 1972, no. 1 (Washington, D.C., Brookings Institution, 1972), pp. 71-121.

Juster, F. Thomas, and Wachtel, Paul, "A Note on Inflation and the Saving Rate," in *Brookings Papers on Economic Activity,* 1972, no. 3, (Washington, D.C.: Brookings Institution, 1972), pp. 765-778.

Kleinewefers, Henner, *Theorie und Politik der Abwertung* (Basel and Tübingen: J.C.B. Mohr, Paul Siebeck, 1969).

Komiya, Ryntaro, "Non-Traded Goods and the Pure Theory of International Trade," *International Economic Review,* 8 (June 1967), pp. 132-152.

Kruger, Anne D., "Balance of Payments Theory," *The Journal of Economic Literature,* 7, no. 1 (1969), pp. 1-26.

Laidler, David E.W., *The Demand for Money: Theories and Evidence,* International Series in Monetary Economics (Scranton, Pennsylvania: International Textbook, 1969).

Levhari, David, and Patinkin, Don, "The Role of Money in a Simple Growth Model," *American Economic Review,* 58 (September 1968), pp. 713-753.

Marty, Alwin, "The Real Balance Effect: An Exercise in Capital Theory," *Canadian Journal of Economics and Political Science,* 30 (August 1964), pp. 364-367.

Mathieson, Donald J. "Traded Goods, Non-Traded Goods, and the Balance of Payments," *International Economic Review,* 14, no. 3 (1973), pp. 615-624.

McDougall, J.W., "Nontraded Goods and the Pure Theory of International Trade," *Studies in International Economics,* ed. I.A. McDougall and R.N. Snape (Amsterdam: North-Holland, 1970).

McKinnon, Ronald J., "Optimum Currency Areas," *American Economic Review,* 53 (September 1963), pp. 717-724.

McKinnon, Ronald J., "Portfolio Balance and International Payments," *Monetary Problems of the International Economy,* ed. Robert A. Mundell and Alexander K. Swoboda (Chicago: University of Chicago Press, 1969), pp. 199-234.

McKinnon, Ronald J., "Money, Growth and the Propensity to Save," *Trade,*

Stability, and Macroeconomics: Essays in Honor of Lloyd A. Metzler, ed. G. Horwich and P.A. Samuelson (New York: Academic Press, 1974), pp. 487-502.

Metzler, Lloyd, "Wealth, Saving and the Rate of Interest," *Journal of Political Economy,* 59 (April 1951), pp. 93-116.

Metzler, Lloyd, "The Process of International Adjustment under Conditions of Full Employment: A Keynesian View," *Readings in International Economics,* ed. Harry G. Johnson and Richard F. Caves (London: Allen & Unwin, 1968), pp. 465-486.

Meyer, Paul A., and Neri, John A., "A Keynes-Friedman Money Demand Function," *American Economic Review,* 65 (September 1975), pp. 610-623.

Michaely, Michael, "Relative Prices and Income-Absorption Approaches to Devaluation: A Partial Reconciliation," *American Economic Review,* 50 (March 1960), pp. 144-147.

Moore, Basil J., *An Introduction to the Theory of Finance: Assetholder Behaviour under Uncertainty* (New York: The Free Press, 1968).

Mundell, Robert A., "The Monetary Dynamics of International Adjustment Under Fixed and Flexible Exchange Rates," *The Quarterly Journal of Economics,* 74 (1960), pp. 227-257.

Mundell, Robert A., "A Theory of Optimum Currency Areas," *American Economic Review,* 51 (November 1961), pp. 657-665.

Mundell, Robert A., *International Economics* (New York: Macmillan, 1968).

Mundell, Robert A., *Monetary Theory: Inflation, Interest and Growth in the World Economy* (Pacific Palisades, Calif.: Goodyear, 1971).

Murphy, J.C., and Das, S.K., "Money Illusion and Balance of Payments Adjustment," *Journal of Political Economy,* 84, no. 1 (1976), pp. 73-82.

Mussa, Michael, "A Monetary Approach to Balance of Payments Analysis," *Journal of Money, Credit and Banking,* 6 (August 1974), pp. 333-351.

Mussa, Michael, "Tariffs and the Balance of Payments: A Monetary Approach," *The Monetary Approach to the Balance of Payments,* ed. Jacob Frenkel and Harry G. Johnson (London: Allen & Unwin, 1976), pp. 187-221.

Mussa, Michael, "The Exchange Rate, the Balance of Payments and Monetary and Fiscal Policy Under a Regime of Controlled Floating," *The Scandinavian Journal of Economics,* 78, no. 2 (1976), pp. 229-248.

Negishi, T., "Approaches to the Analysis of Devaluation," *International Economic Review,* 9, no. 2 (June 1968), pp. 218-227.

Patinkin, Don, *Money, Interest and Prices,* 2nd ed. (New York: Harper & Row, 1965).

Pearce, J.F., "The Problem of the Balance of Payments," *International Economic Review,* 2 (January 1961), pp. 1-28.

Pesek, Boris P., and Saving, Thomas R., *Money, Wealth and Economic Theory* (New York: Macmillan, 1967).

Power, John H., "Price Expectations, Money Illusion, and the Real Balance Effect," *Journal of Political Economy,* 67 (1959), pp. 131-143.

Prais, S.J., "Some Mathematical Notes on the Quantity Theory of Money in an Open Economy," *Staff Papers,* 8 (Washington, D.C.: International Monetary Fund, May 1961), pp. 212-226.

Roper, Don E., "Macroeconomic Policies and the Distribution of the World Money Supply," *Quarterly Journal of Economics,* 85 (February 1971), pp. 119-146.

Rose, Klaus, *Theorie der Aussenwirtschaft,* 6th ed. (Munich: Franz Vahlen, 1976).

Salter, W.E., "Internal and External Balance: The Role of Price and Expenditure Effects," *Economic Record,* 35 (August 1959), pp. 226-238.

Sandler, Todd M., "Devaluation, Capital Flows and the Balance of Payments: A Respecification," *Weltwirtschaftliches Archiv,* 110, no. 2 (1974), pp. 244-258.

Scitovski, Tibor, *Money and the Balance of Payments* (London: Allen & Unwin, 1969).

Sidrauski, Miguel, "Rational Choice and Patterns of Growth in a Monetary Economy," *American Economic Review* (Papers and Proceedings), 57 (May 1967), pp. 534-544.

Sidrauski, Miguel, "Inflation and Economic Growth," *Journal of Political Economy,* 75 (December 1967), pp. 796-810.

Siebke, Jürgen, and Willms, Manfred, "Das Geldangebot in der Bundesrepublik Deutschland. Eine empirische Analyse für die Periode 1958-1968," *Zeitschrift für die gesamte Staatswissenschaft,* 126, no. 1 (1970), pp. 55-74.

Siebke, Jürgen, and Willms, Manfred, *Theorie der Geldpolitik* (Berlin, Heidelberg, New York: Springer, 1974).

Swan, T.W., "Economic Control in a Dependent Economy," *Economic Record,* 36 (March 1960), pp. 51-66.

Swan, T.W., "Longer Run Problems of the Balance of Payments," *The Australian Economy: A Volume of Readings,* ed. Helmut W. Arndt and W. Max Corden (Melbourne: F.W. Cheshire, 1963), pp. 384-395.

Swoboda, Alexander K., "Monetary Approaches to Balance of Payments Theory," *Recent Issues in International Monetary Economics,* ed. Emil M. Claassen and Pascal Salin (Amsterdam: North-Holland, 1976), pp. 3-23.

Swoboda, Alexander K., "Monetary Approaches to the Transmission and Generation of Worldwide Inflation," Discussion Paper, Research Project on National Economic Policy and the International Monetary System (The Graduate Institute of International Studies, Geneva, March 1975).

Tobin, James, "Asset Holdings and Spending Decisions," *American Economic Review* (Papers and Proceedings), 42 (May 1952), pp. 108-123.

Tobin, James, "Money and Economic Growth," *Econometrica,* 33, no. 4 (1965), pp. 671-684.

Tobin, James, "Theory of Portfolio Selection," *The Theory of Interest Rates,* ed. F.H. Hahn and F.P.R. Brechling (London: Macmillan, 1965), pp. 3-51.

Tobin, James, "A General Equilibrium Approach to Monetary Theory," *Journal of Money, Credit and Banking,* 1, no. 1 (1969), pp. 15-29.

Willms, Manfred, "Controlling Money in an Open Economy: The German Case," *Federal Reserve Bank of St. Louis Review,* (April 1971), pp. 10-27.

Willms, Manfred, "Der Monetäre Zahlungsbilanzanpassungsprozess in einem ökonometrischen Modell für die Bundesrepublik Deutschland," *Zeitschrift für Nationalökonomie,* 37, no. 1 (1977), pp. 83-108.

Willms, Manfred, and Masuhr, Klaus, Zahlungsbilanz und Internationaler Monetärer Anpassungsprozess, unpublished paper, Institut für Wirtschaftspolitik Kiel, (Christian-Albrechts-Universität 1976).

Wilson, T., "Effective Devaluation and Inflation," *Oxford Economic Papers* (new series), 28, no. 1 (March 1976), pp. 1-24.

Index

Index

About the Author

Klaus-Walter Riechel, a German national, is an economist with the Central Banking Service of the International Monetary Fund. After completing his studies in economics at the Georg-August University of Göttingen, West Germany, he did his postgraduate studies at the Institut Universitaire de Hautes Etudes Internationales (Graduate Institute of International Studies) in Geneva, Switzerland, and at the Christian-Albrechts University in Kiel, West Germany, from which he received the Ph.D. in economics. Dr. Riechel has taught at both the Institut Universitarie in Geneva and the University of Kiel. He has also worked as an economist in the Economics and Statistics Department of the Organization for Economic Co-operation and Development (O.E.C.D.) in Paris.